KINGS, QUEENS AND KILLERS

Rules of Engagement

LARRY A. YFF

(Book 3 of the "Your View Matters" series)

CHAPTERS

1) B.I.B.L.E. – Basic Instructions Before Leaving Earth Manual   4
2) Women of Royalty
   - Queen Esther   11
   - Ruth   15
   - Herodias   19
3) Killers
   - Samson   22
   - Gideon   29
   - Jephthah   40
   - King David   48
4) King of Kings - Lessons from Jesus' life on Earth   59
5) Prince of Darkness - Lessons from observing Satan's tactics   73
6) Lessons Summary   83
7) Private Matters   95

ACKNOWLEDGEMENTS

I want to thank God for reminding me that "He only has plans for good for those who love Him" and then giving me the confidence, through studying His Word, that I am loved, I am worthy of His plans and I can carry out any plan He has for me.

INTRODUCTION

This book will help you realize the power you have from birth and how to tap into it. It will help you become physical and spiritual warriors who are willing to fight to the death for a worthy cause…the ONLY cause: God's glory and your happiness. There are examples of the successes and failures from people who lived centuries ago that you can learn from. This book walks you through that process to make you the happiest, most successful "you" that you can be.

Private Matters is a section at the back of the book that gives some views on issues that people only share their views on in private (slavery, sex, porn, etc.). Take a look at this list of **Private Matters** topics and see why they make you comfortable in private circles and uncomfortable in public. Your view matters and you should always be confident and able to speak your mind. Your view matters and so do you.

CHAPTER ONE

B.I.B.L.E. – The "Basic Instructions Before Leaving Earth" Manual

You are ahead of the game by starting your search and this book will take you from the point of aimlessly searching for answers to life to executing your every step with precision as you will begin to find true success in everything you do.

You will learn how to enjoy Mondays! You will love rainy days! You will become the rulers of your destiny! "Kill or be killed" will be your motto: you will learn to stand up for God and yourself without hesitation; eliminating anything that tries to kill your dreams!

The lessons from the people in this book will be your guide. If you really want to be successful in everything you do, the instructions in the Bible have to be at the core of every daily decision you make. Learn to control your own destiny and find success. Your journey to becoming true Kings and Queens of your destinies begins now.

Definition of Success

"Keep this Book of the Law always on your lips; meditate on it day and night, so that you may be

careful to do everything written in it. Then you will be prosperous and successful." – Joshua 1:7-9

When you wake up in the morning what's on your mind? I'll bet that being successful is on your agenda. This may mean different things to different people. Just because your version differs from someone else's does not mean it is less important or better. It simply means they are different. In fact, if your views on these ideas are supported with Biblical concepts, all of life's situations you come across will be "win-win" situations without having to force your agenda on someone else.

That verse in the book of Joshua tells us that the level of your success will be determined on how well you focus on scriptures. When you focus on scripture, you are guaranteed to be successful. Using the Bible as your guideline for living will instruct you on how to be a blessing to others. When you operate from that standpoint, success is inevitable because the Bible teaches us how to love and respect God and the people around you. When you invest your time into giving love and respect it comes back to you. That is a successful return on your investment and a high ROI (Return on Investment) no matter how you view it, translates to success.

That's what we all want in life: to be respected and to be a part of something. Why do people join political parties, gangs/mafias, social media groups and professional organizations? It's because we all have a natural desire to be a part of something that is a symbol of respect and success. There is a feeling of love there as well because success in its truest form breeds love.

When you have love, you have a purpose. You are not alone. Love comforts you and gives you a reason to live; while giving you a reason to die. The basic love a parent has for a child is no different than the basic love a gangster has for his gang/mafia. It's no different than the feelings of being a part of something that a constituent or a politician has for his or her political party.

The difference is in how that love is expressed and what the standard is for giving love. The Bible provides us with a standard for giving love and respect that crosses cultural, economic and social lines. It shows us how to give love and how to demand love. Follow those instructions carefully and love, respect and success will always be with you.

Love is a powerful thing. In fact, love is so powerful that entire societies are based on it. How society's leaders define love and the process of getting it shapes cultural, social and economic views. That is why it is so important to have leaders who share the same definition of love and understand that in order to harness that awesome power it means you lead by serving others.

Vision:

"When the wicked rise to power, people go into hiding; but when the wicked perish, the righteous thrive." – Proverbs 28:28

This scripture ties in the role of leaders in determining how a society will function. There are examples all throughout history that show this to be true.

The story of "Moses and the Red Sea" is a classic example where a Ruler can bring peace or calamity to a nation.

The ruling Pharaoh established and had a sense of pride in the power he had set up for himself; becoming a prime example of what the Bible warns us about.

His inability to want to listen to the messages God had delivered through Moses resulted in his land experiencing the Ten Plagues. The people under his rule could have avoided all of those plagues that decimated crops, killed their livestock and killed thousands of men, women, children and babies.

When a country's leaders implement the Bible's definition of leadership, that society will be characterized by economic growth, peace and stability.

That verse in Proverbs tells us the importance of having leaders who know what love is. When the scriptures guide society's leaders…the righteous thrive.

Houses, cars and clothes…

"Why focus on storing up things that lose value and that can be stolen?" – Matthew 6:19

Success for one person may be having a nice house, new cars or a lot of money. Is there anything wrong with this? It depends on your view. The Bible tells us that we should first focus on keeping material things in the right perspective; doing this will keep us from the stress of chasing after these things and tying our value to them.

The value of a house, a car and the dollar ALL change on a daily basis. The values fluctuate based on the laws of supply and demand: if people want (demand) what you have (supply) then the value of your supply will be high; and when nobody wants your product, then the value of it decreases. Supply and demand can be manipulated with crooked legislation and corporate corruption.

This means that if the value of your success changes every day and can be manipulated, then your view and value of yourself changes every day and can be manipulated. Why let yourself go through those changes? Why put yourself in the position where someone else can manipulate your self-worth, peace and your success?

The value of currency changes every day. Its value can be manipulated with the stroke of a pen. If there are greedy people in charge of making international banking laws, they have the ability to control the currency value of one country over another for their benefit.

They say that the second you drive a car off the lot its value decreases. It may become a collector's item 40 years from now; but as of the day of your purchase…its value has gone down and will continue to lose value every minute.

Once again you are basing your value on an item that constantly loses its value. This means that you are going to be spending a considerable amount of time making sure that you keep getting the newest model, the latest model, the most updated model year after year after year. That is your destiny because you will have a need to "update" your value every year that your "personal value related item" loses value.

Here's some perspective: you need a car to drive around and be productive…you don't need a car to prove your value as a human being. You need a house to live in…you don't need a house to prove your value as a human being. You need money to live and be productive…you don't need money to give you value as a human being. See the difference? The Bible doesn't say "don't buy expensive cars and nice houses and don't get rich". What it does say is that if that's what you want go get it.

All through the Bible God told people that He wants us to have nice things and enjoy them. He wanted to lead the Israelites to a Promised Land that was full of the finest things life had to offer. In Genesis 39 we read about how "God was with Joseph so he prospered". In Jeremiah 29 God says "the plans I have are for your good to prosper". In the book of Job we see that Job was a very rich man and after he lost everything during a grueling period of his faith being tested, that God "…made the last part of his life wealthier than the first part of his life." Abraham was extremely wealthy and even had a personal army of more than 300 men. Jacob loved God and through his ups and downs in life, God made it so that he was very wealthy. Even his brother Esau was super rich. God went so far as to say "…bring the full tithes to me and see if I don't open the doors of Heaven and pour out so much blessing that you won't have room to store it…"

The problem comes when we are led to believe that success, power and our ability to both love and be loved are based on what we have physically instead of spiritually.

You have to love God more than you love material things and that's the bottom line. In Matthew 6:24 Jesus flat out says that it's impossible to love God and love money. They are polar opposites. God is forever. Money is not. Money is simply the tool that allows us to show how much we love God, ourselves and other people.

The Bible provides us with plenty of examples of how people used love, power and money the right way…and some who didn't. Here are their stories:

CHAPTER TWO

Women of Royalty – Lessons from Queen Esther, Ruth and Herodias

QUEEN ESTHER

When Esther[1] was young, the King in the country where she lived was on a mission: he was looking for a wife to be Queen. He sent his royal staff out and instructed them to bring back the most beautiful young females in his kingdom. She was chosen as a candidate. Here is the story of her rise through the ranks to become Queen:

"God's Timing" rule

As far as we know, Esther never had dreams of becoming a Queen when she grew up. God's timing can propel you into a career that you never dreamed of. We have all heard stories of famous people who never imagined they would be traveling the world and having as much impact on society as they do.

---
[1] The Book of Esther

Sometimes it was because of their poor upbringing and other times it had more to do with the views of the society they were born into. Either way, none of those factors have an impact on your destiny. You were born at just the right time and it usually isn't clear until after you've had a chance to slow down and look back.

Esther was no exception to "God's Timing" rule. She was a young, pretty girl at the time that the King just so happened to be looking for someone like that to be Queen.

If she had been born later on in life, she would not have had the same opportunity. And if she was born years earlier, she would have also missed this opportunity.

God's timing has a way of combining your assets with your destiny. There is no template for what that combination is and that's the beauty!! You don't know what your destiny holds and how to use what you have until you tune in to God's Word!! Every day could be that day where you step into your destiny!

In Esther's case, she was able to use the assets of her age and beauty to get her in the door. Don't ever count yourself out because you think you are too young or too old or don't have a certain look! Leave that way of thinking to those who don't understand how God works. *You* just continue to study the Bible and understand that whatever you have is exactly what you need to fulfill your destiny and anything you need on this path, will be provided to you as you stay plugged in to His Word.

Once she was in, God gave her the next tool that she would need to open the next door: proper instruction. All of the queen candidates had to go through a one year beauty-regimen taught by highly-trained, royal staff to school the young girls on how to present themselves and highlight their natural, feminine beauty.

Her ability to take advice from her instructors is what elevated her from candidate to Queen. *Who* instructs you is just as important as *what* their instructions are. As you begin to understand how God works, you will not feel limited in any way if you don't have access to proper instruction because you will know that God said in the Bible[2] "...I will put my law in their minds and write it on their hearts." Knowing that we all have equal access to God's instructions because it's in us at birth means that your chances of achieving success are just as good as anyone else's. The advantage goes to *anyone* who recognizes this scripture.

When it was Esther's turn to go in front of the King, she only said what her instructor's told her to say. That good advice was recognized by the King, as planned by her instructors, and that was the start of her becoming Queen.

<u>Fulfilling Your Destiny</u>

---

[2] Jeremiah 31:33

Once God's timing begins to guide you on your path, you will become more and more aware of your destiny. As Esther began to see God's hand in her life, her confidence grew and she was able to use what she learned on her path to help her fulfill her destiny.

On your path is where you learn the tools and skills that you need once you arrive at your destiny. The path is a crucial time where you have to pay attention and understand how God works. Esther used what she learned about using her natural beauty, her knowledge of royal behavior and her ability to listen to good advice to save thousands of lives in her role as Queen.

Once again we see God's timing at work: she just happened to be a wise, Jewish Queen at the exact point and time in history when her position was what was needed to prevent the genocide of the Jewish culture.

Some of the King's officials decided they would wipe out the Jews that lived in that area. Queen Esther found out from her uncle who she kept in contact with. Because of her position, she was able to go to the King and ask him for a favor. His first thing was to let her know she could have anything up to half of his kingdom.

Right there, if she had climbed the ranks with bad advice from greedy people, she could have opted for the wealth; but since she had learned on her way to the top to listen to wise counsel she was able to stick to the game plan.

She tells the King about the plan and that she knows who the guilty ones are and she wants them taken care of. The King grants her request. The thing that is amazing about this is that in order to grant her request, the King had to kill one of his own royal staff members. This is after he was just now made aware that she was Jewish! She had to hide this fact because she was in a foreign country.

Her story ends with the Jewish culture and tradition of her time being saved and her uncle being rewarded for giving her good advice. He was given a position that made him second in command; outranked only by the King. By following good advice, she was able to be a blessing to both her culture and her family in a major way and carry out her destiny.

RUTH

Another woman who was given a lot of attention in the Bible was Ruth. She never had an official royal title; however, she became the female who started the royal bloodline of King David, and as you know, Jesus was a direct descendant of that line.[3] Here's her story:

Faith in God and her "person of influence."

---

[3] Ruth 4:16-22

A lady named Naomi had two sons. Their wives were named Ruth and Orpah. When the two sons died, Naomi decided to go back to her homeland dejected. Her daughter-in-law Ruth decided to go with her; while the other one stayed.

Naomi tried to convince Ruth to stay as well but Ruth remained loyal to her. Ruth had seen something in Naomi that she wanted. She told Naomi that she was going with her and that Naomi's God would be her God, etc.

Ruth must have recognized the God in Naomi and decided that was what she wanted. She had a respect for God that led her to believe that being in the company of her mother-in-law, a follower of God, would be enough for her. This shows her level of faith and spirituality. It also showed her level of independence: no man, no money and she is about to go live in a foreign country…yet she had faith in God and herself that she would somehow be fine.

Timing and Productivity

The next thing we learn about this young lady is her willingness to be productive. When she got to her new homeland, she didn't set about to find a man. Her priority was to be productive and she was not too proud to get dirty. She told Naomi that she was going to go work picking up leftover grain in the fields.

Her focus was not on what other people might think or worrying about getting paid what she was worth. She stayed focused on being productive. With her willingness to be humble, she caught the attention of the owner of the field that she had chosen.

We have to talk about and recognize "God's Timing" rule in Ruth's life. They arrived at the time of the harvest. In those days, the primary forms of income were from farming and raising livestock. Her opportunity to meet her husband and continue on to her destiny hinged on timing.

She was able to find work immediately because it was the harvest season. This is where her future husband (and great-grandfather to King David) noticed her. If she had arrived before or after the time of harvesting, this opportunity would not have existed.

That's why it's important to understand that God has plans for your good and all you have to do is focus on the everyday lessons. As a Christian, your advantage is that you don't have to stress about where you are at in life at any given time. You know that you are tuned in to God's Word and that, as you have seen, His timing will be perfect. You are free to enjoy each day and the lessons it brings because you understand these lessons will be put into play once you arrive at your destiny!

Proper Procedure

The same way that Esther received and followed good advice is the same way Ruth acted. All of Ruth's actions put her in the position where she was noticed by her future husband, Boaz. Those actions got her noticed…they did not guarantee entrance into the next leg of her destiny.

You never know what lesson is going to be the one to open the next door. To me, that is absolutely exciting and makes me look forward to each day! Knowing that I have been working on an area of my life and that once God believes I have proven myself with it that the next door will open! It doesn't get more exciting than that!!

Her mother-in-law Naomi counseled her on how to approach Boaz. That's important to note that. There is proper protocol for every situation. Ruth was fortunate enough to have someone show her what protocol was for landing a gentleman of Boaz's character.

Naomi recognized the process and instructed Ruth on how to present herself. She did as she was instructed and Boaz could not resist because he was a man of protocol as well.

How you present yourself is a common determining factor on how your relationships will be. Ladies, if you show a lot of skin to attract a man, then you will attract men who want to see a lot of skin. In this case, she presented herself as a compliment to him. She came as an employee and he was an employer. She approached him in accordance to the protocol and he in turn went through the proper channels to make sure nobody else had a customary claim to her so that he could marry her.

Her story ends with her getting married and having a son who would eventually be King David's grandfather. At the same time, she was able to be a blessing to Naomi because Boaz did what was necessary to allow Naomi to be a part of this newly formed family and carry on her family name.

HERODIAS

This next female is a classic example of how a person who is in a position of leadership can give terrible advice with devastating results. In this instance "that person" was Herodias. She was the King's sister-in-law and used her access to power in a devious manner. She is better known as "the Royal Femme Fatale". Here's how she got her "title":

Oh, what a tangled web we weave, when at first we practice to deceive…[4]

There was a King named Herod. He had a sister-in-law named Herodias. The details aren't exact as to what did or did not happen; but what is clear is that King Herod and she had a thing for each other.

---

[4] Sir Walter Scott

Unfortunately for John the Baptist, he openly spoke against it. He did so to the point where King Herod had him locked up and Herodias wanted to kill him. If she had the authority to, she would have done it; but since she did not have that type of authority, she would have to wait for her opportunity to make her move.

Her moment to carry out her devious desire came about at a party. King Herod threw a party and Herodias had her daughter dance for the King. He is so happy he tells her in front of everyone that she can have whatever she likes.

She turns to her mother and asks what she should wish for and her mother tells her to ask for the head of John the Baptist. The daughter tells the King that she wants the head of John the Baptist and since everyone heard the King say he would grant her a wish, he was obligated to do it.

He makes the call to the prison and has John beheaded. The head is then placed on a platter and delivered to Herodias.

John's death was the result of King Herod and Herodias' actions. Neither of them wanted to admit their sin and decided to take action to cover it up. Many of us have been in this situation. We know we are doing wrong and would rather cover it up or if we are in the position to do so, try and use legislation to make our sinful actions "legal".

Here is where the transfer of generational wisdom can play a significant role in our lives. We see that the daughter did exactly what the mother asked. We don't know whether or not the daughter knew the rationale behind her mother's request. All we do know is that her "person of influence" transferred to her a way of thinking that was based on deception that cost a good man his life.

We see a common theme again: who you get your advice from is just as important as what the advice is. The Bible gives us solid advice about sex and relationships straight from God. That advice is based on love and respect. Love and respect do not deceive.

CHAPTER THREE

Killers – Lessons from Samson, Gideon, Jephthah, and King David

SAMSON

Samson, one of Israel's rulers, was blessed with superhuman, physical strength. He used this strength to kill and murder people on more than one occasion. In the situations documented in the Bible, they were all related to him having a problem with a female. In the end, God had a purpose for all of this mayhem and chaos. Here is the story of those murderous events:

A killer with a purpose.

The life and times of Samson, [5]ruler of Israel for approximately 20 years, is riddled with murder and female problems.

The first example of this we see is when he is a young man. He notices a young, Philistine lady and he decides to marry her. In these days it was customary to

---

[5] Judges 16:31

have a 7-day marriage festival. Samson and his dad go to her city and begin the celebration. When the people saw him, they instantly assigned 30 men to be his companions.

He tells his new "friends" a joke and lets them know that if they can tell him the answer before the week-long celebration is up, he will give each of them a new set of clothes. If they can't guess it, they owe him 30 new outfits.

For three days they can't figure it out. They go to his fiancé and threaten to kill her and her dad if she doesn't get the answer out of him. The next four days she nags and begs for the answer. She tells him he doesn't love her. He finally gives in and she runs to tell his companions the answer.

When they give him the answer, he knew she had told. As a man of his word, he had to give each of his 30 companions a new set of clothes. He goes to a nearby city and kills 30 men, takes their clothes off and brings them to his 30 companions as payment.

Disgusted, he leaves the city and his fiancé behind and returns to his parent's home. With him gone, one of his companions marries her.

Sometime later he decides to return. When he arrives at his "wife's" house, her father tells Samson that she is married and he isn't welcome at his house anymore unless he marries her sister.

Samson gets mad and goes out and catches 300 foxes. He takes them two-by-two and ties their tales together with a lit torch in the middle. They run loose in the fields, burning up entire crops of grain, vineyards and olive orchards.

This was extremely detrimental to the local economy because it was at the time of harvest. This means that the crops were all ready to be harvested and sold at market. By him destroying these crops, he decimated the entire harvest causing massive loss of income.

They get mad and find out he did it. In retaliation, they burn his fiancé and her father alive. This in turn gets him mad and he attacks and kills many of them with his bare hands.

Some of Samson's people come to him and ask him to turn his self in because if he doesn't the Philistines are prepared to attack them. He agrees and they tie his hands up. As they approach the Philistines with their prisoner, he breaks free, picks up a jawbone of a donkey and kills 1000 Philistines.

The next situation we hear about is when Samson travels to a city and goes to bed with a local prostitute. When the locals hear about it, they decide he will be vulnerable and plan to attack him early in the morning. Samson decides to leave in the middle of the night and unknowingly avoids the trap.

He couldn't get enough of the Philistine women and eventually meets and falls in love with another one named Delilah. When the Philistine men heard about it, they approached Delilah and offered to give her a lot of money if she could persuade him to tell her the source of his strength.

She asks him for the secret to his strength three separate times. Each time he lies to her. She did exactly what he told her to do once he fell asleep to make him weak and each time after she did what he said she would try and set him up. The Philistines would be hiding, waiting to get him and she would say "Samson! The Philistines are here" and he would wake up and break loose.

Finally she plays the "how can you say you love me when you keep lying to me" card, and he gives in and tells her the truth. The Philistines are able to capture and tie him up this time. They gouge his eyes out and make him perform "chain gang" type labor.

The Philistines decide to have a celebration on finally catching the great "Philistine Killer" and at the party they have him on display and make fun of him.

Samson, completely humiliated and humbled, asks God to give him strength just one more time so that he could get revenge on them and kill some more Philistines. God gives him strength and Samson pushes against two of the big, stone pillars, knocking them out of position. As the ceilings and walls come crashing down, Samson and more than a thousand party-goers all die.

We learn that God wanted to use Samson to kill the Philistines[6]. This nation was always at odds with the

---

[6] Judges 14:4

Israelites and this was a way of being a thorn in their side. During the time of these events, the Philistines were actually ruling over the Israelites and God used these events of Samson's life for a season as a way of harassing and killing them, potentially for having the Israelites under their rule.

The mind of a killer.

What made this Man of God resort to violence and killing so easily and what lessons are in it for us?

Disrespect towards his parents is one factor. This often leads to extremely selfish behavior and temper-tantrums when the child doesn't get his or her way and that in turn leads to corruption in business dealings and the justice system as the child becomes an adult and wants to get his or her way.

Samson was no exception. When he is at the age where he wants to get married we read that he sees a young lady and tells his parents to "go get her for me" even after his parents object and say that this girl isn't the one for him. They do what he said. He was used to getting his way. When a parent says "no" and you fight back and *make* your parents do what you say…there is a respect problem that needs to be addressed.

The natural, physical chemistry in males is another factor. Males have testosterone and are built for physical activity and aggression. When that natural aggression goes unchecked, a young man will try and figure out on his own how to harness it.

There is evidence of this in nature particularly when you deal with elephants and lions. When you see the young males in those animal societies that are the most dysfunctional members, it's usually because there is no head male to guide them. They are generally violent and extremely short tempered.

In Samson's case, he realized he had superhuman strength and he used that to lash out and hurt people when he got mad. Without a male presence to tell him the best way to harness those physical urges, killing and violence became his go-to options.

You can never discount the natural power of seduction that a female has over a male. This was very obvious as Samson allowed himself to stumble and get tripped up time on at least three major instances. The first instance of him showing a weakness for seduction was when he saw a female and went against his parent's advice and forced them to comply with what he wanted.

The second instance was when he killed thirty men to pay off a bet. He got into that fit of anger because he gave in to his fiancé so she would stop nagging and telling him that he must not love her.

The final act, the one that led to his capture and ultimately his death, was because he gave away the source of his strength to his deceitful wife. All she had to do was continue to press him and let him know that he couldn't possibly love her because he lied to her and he gave away the secret ingredient to the sauce.

The instances where those females held that power over him revealed another possible clue to his violent tendencies: frustration from not taking responsibility for his actions. When his first fiancé kept pressing him for answers, he had the option to simply not tell her or decide at the early stage of their relationship that she may not be the one.

The incident with his wife Delilah that led to him being captured was no different. After he lied to her the first time and he saw that she wanted the answer to his strength so that she could set him up to be killed he should have left her. He decided to stay. In fact, she tried to set him up three times and each time he stayed with her.

In the end we read that God would give Samson the strength to carry out these killing sprees for a purpose. This happened even though they were the direct result of his lack of insight and poor judgment.

Oddly enough, Samson's dying request to kill more Philistines was once again given the green light by God. This shows us how God operates in many different ways and what we may think is a life of chaos and confusion is actually a well-orchestrated life of purpose.

GIDEON

He stepped into his destiny as cautious as a cat. His first days were full of doubt and fear. In the end, he made the list as a skillful killer/warrior who relentlessly eliminated all competition. Being a warrior was not on his mind. It took God approaching and guiding him to realize his potential and leading him into his position as one of the greatest warriors that ever lived. He is the real-life warrior behind the movie "300"[7]:

Career Change 101

Many of us have been in situations where we feel stuck. We start to get impatient and a lot of times, we make decisions that seem necessary at the time but have serious consequences in the end. And usually it comes from anxiety: When will this situation be over? When will I find a new job? When will I get rich?

In every Bible story we read, we are able to see the beginning and the ending. It's as though God has a plan and we get to see it unfold as we watch other people's lives; but when it's our life it's a little harder to just sit back and experience it.

It's what we call "Monday night quarterbacking" or "hindsight is 20/20 vision". We say that because once a

---

[7] Judges 7:7

situation is over we are able to look back and see how it happened and what we could have *potentially* done to change the outcome.

The more you study how God moves, the more you will be at peace with your situation because you know that at the exact, right time your situation will be over because God has a plan for your life and you have seen how God keeps His promise of having "plans for good for those who love Me."

Gideon's career-change came during a time when the Israelites, once again, were under the control of some other nation because they were focusing on evil and not on following God's law. In fact, his career-change, as usual, came at the exact time that was needed so that Israel could get out from under the Midianite's rule...and he wasn't even looking for a new career.

Israel had been under foreign rule for seven years when God came to Gideon to inform him that he was going to start a new career. His response was similar to ours.

An angel of God came and called him a mighty warrior and said that God was with him. Gideon's first response was that there was no way God could be with him because his people were in bad shape.

There is another similarity with us. How many times have we been in a situation that we think is unfair and since we think it's unfair we either blame God or say that God left us for dead? These negative views that we all get at times are career-killers. They are depressing. They can often times make us feel like we'd be better off dead than living.

Your view matters in situations like this! You can look at the world and say, "This world is terrible and there is no way God can be real because if He was, all the bad stuff wouldn't be happening." That is where you need to realize God is smarter than you or me and that every situation is part of a master plan by the creator of this universe.

The choice is yours. You can either: 1) doubt God and allow yourself to get depressed, miserable and angry and that in turn will turn your entire life upside down, or 2) you can realize that there is a plan in the making and that it is a good one and that *maybe* God might even want to use you in a leadership role for some part of it.

Several stories in the Bible are there to help us see how "everything works out for the good of those who love God." The Israelites were slaves or under foreign rule several times. Each time that they decided to act right, God approached someone He knew could get the job done AND gave that person EVERYTHING he or she needed for a successful career move.

We have heard people say that they wouldn't do something "unless Jesus Himself came and told me to." It seems like that would be all it takes, but as we move deeper into Gideon's story, sometimes it may take a "Q and A" session before we do what we are supposed to. That's the position we find Gideon in. Let's take a look at the career-move essentials that Gideon focused on during his session:

1. Who referred this position? When the angel addressed him by his new title as "mighty warrior" and said that God was with him, he didn't believe in his "new position" because it was backed by God and he felt like God had abandoned him. Because of his issue with abandonment, he didn't accept the position yet. **Hindsight 20/20 Tip:** God promised He would never leave you. This means even when you feel like your world is falling apart you need to have faith that you have the power to correct it! If you are in a situation on account of someone else's actions, you know since you understand how God works, your situation has a time limit and a lesson. You may have gotten yourself into a bad situation by making bad decisions; and if so you can get yourself out of it by making good ones. Accepting an offer from God to change careers is always going to be a good decision.
2. What qualifications does the position require? The angel then told him to "use the strength you currently have and save Israel." This made him really not want to take the position because, as he explained to the angel, "I come from a family with now power and in that family I am the one who hasn't done anything with my life." **Hindsight 20/20 Tip:** It doesn't matter if you are rich or poor or if you feel like you haven't made anything of your life. God has a way of knowing you better than you know yourself and when He calls you it's for something great. Don't EVER doubt yourself. In all of these stories, none of them appeared to be

extra special or privileged. You have the same ability to be used by God for greatness at any time and in any place as the next person. You will see how Gideon doubted himself and God still was able to use him and make him known as a mighty warrior-leader.

3. Show me the money!! The angel now tells Gideon that he, the angel, has Gideon's back and that he, Gideon, will kill all of the Midianites. Gideon's response is to ask for a sign. He wanted a guarantee that the person in front of him making the offer is a representative of God and that he will have the success that this rep promised. He goes inside and comes out with a tray of food. The angel touches the plate of food with his walking stick and it instantly starts on fire. In the amazement and confusion of the moment…the angel disappears. Now he is ready to make that career-move.

Hindsight 20/20 Tip: It's okay to ask for a sign from God. This may be a controversial point, but I believe that every story in the Bible has a lesson for us on how God acts and how we are supposed to act. This act of asking for a sign as a means of a confidence booster is not limited to the Old Testament. In the New Testament[8] Jesus says, "Ask and it will be given to you….everyone who asks and seeks will receive and find…"

First Day Jitters

---

[8] Matthew 7:7 - 12

You may think that after all the signs and the back and forth with the questions and the guarantees and the actual acceptance by Gideon of God's offer that he becomes a full-fledged warrior. If you think that then you are right and wrong. "Right" because he does become a full-fledged warrior; but "wrong" because it still takes some time and convincing on God's part to get Gideon to where he needs to be mentally in order to be a mighty warrior.

Without getting too deep into detail, God basically asks Gideon to do something. He does it, but he does it in the middle of the night because he was afraid of his family and the people in the town.

There are a couple things from his first act on his way to becoming a warrior that you can learn from:

1. Take action: God asked Gideon to do something and even though he was scared he pushed through the fear and did it! In the verses telling us of his first act as a "mighty warrior" it says "…because he was afraid of his family and townspeople, he did it at night time rather than in the day…" Taking that first step against fear is often the first lesson we need to learn. If you feel in your heart about a certain path that God has placed in your heart: take action. Learn to conquer fear or fear, all by itself, will kill your dreams and your destiny.
2. Just because you may feel like you have a calling from God does NOT mean you will automatically

have the acceptance of your family and those around you: He took a stand against the spiritual practices of his father[9] *while* he was living in his father's house. That takes heart! That takes more courage and faith in one's self and in God than in any situation! Those are essential for warrior training! God will help you take baby steps to get you to where you need to be and this is another classic example. Gideon needed to learn to stand up for himself and step into his own destiny even if it meant standing up to his dad.
3. You can still live with fear when it comes time to take the consequences of taking your first step: After taking his first step of faith, which was an act that completely defiled the spirituality of his father and the people in his town, he was scared to some degree. It says when the town people came to confront him at his dad's house about what he had done to the statue of their god…he did not come out.
4. Respect: When the angry mob came to question Gideon about tearing down the statue, he found support from an unlikely source: his dad. When you take a stand, people recognize it and support may come from the most unlikely of places. In this case, even though Gideon had torn down his dad's statue to the god named Baal, his dad still used logic and rational to support his son. You may find that the people you think would support you won't and on the flipside, you may find that the people you thought would be against you will openly support you. On

---
[9] Judges 7:25

your quest to fulfill your destiny, don't underestimate or overlook anyone! You never know who your next enemy or ally will be.

He publicly stepped into his warrior role by going through the land, calling for the people to bear arms and prepare for battle.

Even though he is now in the public eye and people are following him, he still wasn't 100% confident in his new role. Once again, he called on God and asked God for a sign to make sure that he was really going to win the war and free the Israelites. God gave him the sign. Gideon goes back and asks God one more time for another sign. God gave him that sign as well.

Sometimes we are like that. We know God has a plan for us in a certain field and when the opportunity presents itself, we may be excited but we still don't go full speed ahead. There may be doubts about our ability to lead or we may question how can we actually carry out our destiny when we are poor or the "wrong" race or have a criminal record.

It's okay to ask God for a sign. It's YOUR destiny and you have a right to come to God and ask of Him whatever you want regarding your next moves. We see many great men and women of God who may have questions and just want that assurance from God before they actually stepped into their destiny.

Gideon's 300

All the men that he gathered to do battle with the Midianites was around 32,000. God told Gideon that he had too many soldiers. He wanted to make sure that the Israelites would not be able to claim the victory on their own might and manpower.

That's important to remember: When you are stepping into a "God destiny" you are doing it to 1) give glory to God, and 2) enjoying the earthly benefits of doing His will. It's easy to forget about how God has brought you into your destiny if can point to some worldly method that propelled you.

There are tons of people who are quick to say, "I did it by working two jobs and getting my degree and never accepting defeat as an option." How many times do you see famous people say, "I couldn't have made all these millions of dollars without FOLLOWING GOD'S LAWS."

I highlighted the last part because people are quick to recognize a spiritual side to their accomplishments and are even quick to give an honorable mention to God…but very few say HOW God helped them or HOW they had to follow God's laws. Their shout of "honorable mention to God" is usually followed up with all the people who helped them get there and all the lucky breaks and hard work THEY did to get where they are.

God understands this and He has some pretty unique ways of getting us to realize His hand in our success. Here, He tells Gideon to go into battle with only 300 men. When you go up against an army of thousands and defeat them, it's pretty hard to chalk it up to your skill alone. You will HAVE to recognize God's awesome power and presence in the battle.

God also understands that even when we have entered into our destinies and God has given us signs, we still may need a little encouragement. God sensed that Gideon may have been a little unsure still and told him, "If you are scared, sneak down to the edge of the enemy camp and listen to their topic of discussion as proof that I am with you and you will be victorious."

Gideon goes down to the edge of the camp and overhears two men talking. The one man tells of a dream he had and the other one says, "That dream means that God is with the Israelite named Gideon and he will come with swords and defeat the Midianites."

With this newly gained confidence, Gideon returned to where his 300 men were sleeping. He tells them to get up and get ready for battle.

Here's the kicker: They had swords but their first weapon of choice would be trumpets and torches! Each man had a trumpet in one hand and a torch that was hidden inside of clay jars. When they approached the enemy, they simply blew their trumpets and smashed their jars. The sudden blare of the trumpets and the sight of all the torches sent the enemy army into confusion.

The enemy force was a coalition from different nations. In the confusion and chaos they all began to turn on each other.

With the opposing army in chaos, Gideon and his 300 began their pursuit of the fleeing enemy, killing them by the hundreds, until they caught up with the two kings and their bodyguards that they were chasing. Gideon then personally killed both of the kings with his sword. That act was the sign of the battles' end and that Israel was now free from the rule of the Midianites.

Because of this victory, there was peace in the land for the next 40 years that Gideon was alive. He died an old man of natural causes.

Gideon became a great Man of God even though he thought very little of himself in the beginning. He was insecure and operated out of fear. He had no self-confidence in his abilities and on several occasions he came to God for reassurance.

Many of us feel like we are operating from a position of disadvantage…but we're not!! We are operating from the position God wants us to operate from and with the skills we have. We will step into our destiny at His time with His support. If that is what we seek and if that is the destiny we want…like Gideon, we have to recognize God's hand in our life and just take that first step and we will not fail!

JEPHTHAH

In this story, Jephthah was a great Israelite warrior that saved the day when they were under attack by several foreign countries. His arrival on the scene came years after Gideon was called by God for the same purpose, basically under the same circumstances: The Israelites had strayed and God allowed them to be under foreign control for 18 years. His willingness to do battle with anyone and his loyalty to his God and his country gave him victory over his enemies and led to the saddest death of a child that was ever recorded in the Bible[10]. Here is this warrior's story:

Warrior, please come home!

Israel had turned away from God so God allowed foreign countries to attack and have their way with them for years. Eventually they would repent and ask God to save them.

In their search for the best warrior to lead them, Jephthah's name came up. The leaders of Israel went to find him and asked him to lead their army and in return he would be their leader.

They had to find him because he was on the run. His dad had kids with his wife and also with a prostitute. Jephthah's mother was the prostitute. His brothers told him

---

[10] Judges 10 and 11

he would not get any inheritance because of that and didn't claim him as a legitimate brother or family member. They went so far as to chase him out of his homeland.

Some of us have been in similar situations. Have you ever felt like you didn't fit in with your family? Maybe you feel like you get treated unfairly because you are the youngest or the oldest or a stepchild or a foster child. Here's the thing: if you understand how God works those feelings, whether real or perceived, can't stop your destiny! How do I know that? By looking at stories of how God operates and understanding that the way He operated back in Bible times is the same way He operates now!

In this case, he is called back by the leaders of the land he had to run from because of his skill as a warrior. The fate of his homeland depended on him.

Boundaries and Expectations

There are times where the same people who rejected you may need you. Understanding how to act in those situations is paramount. You can either reject their request because you are still angry with them *or* you can learn to step into your destiny by learning how to not operate in your feelings.

Jephthah had confidence in his ability to lead and put his emotions aside. He did this by having a conversation with them and established clear boundaries and expectations before dealing with them again.

You may need to have a conversation with an elderly parent in need of help that you feel rejected you when you were younger. Answer that call for help from that family member that you thought hated you and have a conversation. Our nature is to love and help and when you are able to operate in line with that, you will be able to stay on track with your destiny. Look at how Jephthah handled his rejection.

The first thing he did was to establish some boundaries. He made sure that they knew that it was on them for the separation and that they came to him and that the past would remain in the past. He needed that to be acknowledged before he could proceed with the conversation.

Once that was agreed upon, he wanted to make sure there was no more miscommunication moving forward so he asked them if they were telling him the truth about his reward for leading them to battle. They agreed and sealed it before God. Those conversations allowed everyone to operate as equals.

If you notice, his faith and loyalty to God is what gave him the assurance that everything would be ok: he basically made them swear to God in front of God that they would acknowledge their end of the bargain as long as he took care of his end. His expectations going into battle were that he would win because He followed protocol and asked God to honor his actions.

Military Mindset

Craving an extensive knowledge of battlefield and military history is reserved for true warriors and students of warfare. Jephthah is a true warrior and a man with his military education is exactly what was needed to see a victory.

His first order of business was to be political. He sent word to the enemy asking them what was the basis for the attack. The enemy king responded by saying that the land where the Israelites were living at used to be under *his* country's rule and he was coming to take it back.

The past can be hard to forget especially when your identity is tied to a culture. Israel was under attack because of some events that had happened 300 years prior.

As a student of history, Jephthah sends a messenger out again to the enemy king and explains in great detail how Israel got to be in that land. He told how God lead Israel out of Egypt and how God gave instructions for them to ask permission to pass through the land of the king of each land they passed through until they arrived to their own land…the land that God had promised them.

He then went on to explain why Israel was justified in being there and wanting to defend that right: our God lead us here and we will fight to keep what our God has given us just like you would fight to keep what your god has given you.

But he took it a step further and let the enemy know that this is a spiritual warfare situation and that "we should let our God and your god sort it out in their own way…we don't need to go to war".

His rational debate, warnings and attempts to avoid military conflict fell on deaf ears. The enemy king didn't want to hear anything Jephthah proposed; making war inevitable.

"Fatal Request"

It's time for combat. Jephthah does what he was accustomed to and makes sure God knows his plans and asks for God's support; but this time he adds a little extra to his request and tells God, "If you give me this great victory, I will sacrifice to you whatever comes out of my house when I return home victorious."

There have been times in our lives where we want something so badly that we agree to something we probably shouldn't have. I know I have taken on debt that I shouldn't have only because I was caught up in the moment or felt like I had to have some item right then and there or the world would end.

Some of you may have also been in situations where you felt prompted, pushed or persuaded into buying a car, boat or house that you can't really afford. Maybe love was the culprit behind some of your purchases. Regardless, you are now, as the Bible says, "the slave to the lender".

Society says that you can't be successful unless you have a degree and that wrong belief, even though there is a lot of truth in that line of thinking, has led some of us to feel "forced" into taking on staggering amounts of student debt.

Whatever the reason or rationale was, in these common scenarios you may have found yourself legally bound and accountable to a bank, or a friend or the government.

Jephthah made a deal and knew that he would be 100% accountable to God. No bailouts. No backing out. No filing bankruptcy. Maybe it was that Jephthah wanted acknowledgement by his peers and family that made him add his *demande fatale*. Whatever the reason, he had to stick to it. He was loyal to God and his profession and in this case with heart-breaking results.

The battle starts and he leads the army into victory, demolishing 20 enemy cities before it was all over. He returns home victorious and happy until his little girl runs out the door to great him!!

Jephthah is crushed!! After explaining to his daughter the arrangement that he promised God, his daughter accepts her fate. She agrees that it's only right because God did His part and gave him the military victory.

She now has one request of her own and says to her dad, "I will die young and never experience marriage. Please let my friends and I have two months to roam the hillside and mourn."

He allows her that time. When she returns, he sacrifices her to God like he promised. She was an only child…

"Give and Take" *NOT* "Take and Take."

We are quick to call on God when something goes wrong. Once our prayers are answered, and the fire is put out, we have a tendency to go back to business as usual. Is that fair to God? It doesn't feel good when we are in situations where we are always the "giver" and never the "receiver"…so why put God through that?

Walking the Christian life means that we follow God's laws and that requires that we study who is giving the laws and then studying the laws.

Walking the Christian life means that we are accountable to God…not the other way around. We are supposed to have that warrior mentality that makes us want to fight for what is right.

We need to treat God how we want Him to treat us. That means that if we always expect and even demand that He keeps His word, we should keep ours to Him as well.

THAT is the type of commitment and loyalty to God that we need to have!! We always want God to do this or that for us; but when we are asked to simply follow His laws, we find all types of excuses and reasons why it doesn't make sense UNTIL we find ourselves in a jam again and go crying to God.

Teach a child the way she should go…

If you notice, when he told his daughter what he had promised to God, she didn't hesitate or complain.

He showed her how to respect God with his actions to the point where she absolutely understood the necessity to honor what you say to God. She must have seen God's hand in her dad's life prior to this instance for her to accept her fate based on her dad's word to God. We know this because she basically let her dad know that since he gave God his word and God did his part, she would expect nothing short of him keeping his word to God no matter what was said.

Jephthah, you ARE the Ultimate Warrior!

KING DAVID

Killing was a way of life for King David. He began by killing animals that would attack his sheep; then he became known as the "Great Killer of Men". Here's how his lessons learned as a killer led him to become the King:

Overlooked and Rejected

If David had to recall his journey to his destiny, I believe there would have been a lot of crying and reliving feelings of rejection.

When the prophet Samuel came as instructed by God to anoint one of Jesse's sons as the next King, David was completely overlooked. His dad didn't even present him to the prophet. He lined up seven of his sons without even a thought of David. In fact, his dad had completely forgotten about the fact that David could even be in the running to be anointed until Samuel asked him if he had any other sons.

Have you ever felt like nobody would miss you if you decided to quit your job or move to another state? You are not alone. David's own dad didn't miss him. You may not even know who is rejecting you or talking about you behind your back and it doesn't matter.

In Psalm 118, David writes "the stone that the builder has rejected has become the cornerstone". He also mentions rejection several times in the book of Psalm when he asks God "Why have You rejected us?" And in the next moment he mentions over 40 times how much he trusts in God and loves Him.

This shows us how much David was like us. We have all had those times where we wonder why God rejected us; as well as the times where we thank God for being with us.

That is one of the main reasons I believe God favored David through all his good and bad times: he was ultimately concerned with how he stood in God's eyes with very little concern about what people thought about him.

As Christians we don't have to worry about being rejected by people. What they say doesn't matter and we have proof. David was overlooked and rejected by his own family but not by God and that recognition by God was all that was needed in his life.

David didn't even have to do anything special to get noticed. He didn't have to tell people how good he was. He didn't have to ask people to accept him. His destiny wasn't tied up in the connections he made. He had an understanding and love for God and that was all he needed.

We know that God had plans for David and it was David's faithfulness to God that helped him come into his destiny as a King.

<u>Do what you're good at.</u>

David's first notable step towards greatness was based on him simply being himself. The king at this time, King Saul, was affected by wild mood swings. He was told that the best remedy was to have someone play music from a harp for him. This advice was followed up with his royal staff members suggesting that he ask David to play for him.

Do you see how that works? When you focus on doing what you are good at, people will take notice without you forcing the situation. David was summoned to the King's palace and performed so well that the King asked David's dad was it okay if David stayed and remained employed with the royal staff.

People have a tendency to think that the only way to get noticed is to get noticed. That's not how it works if you want to operate in the God system. In this system, you already know that God notices you and that He has plans for your good. All you have to do is continue to thrive in whatever environment you find yourself in because you know that each stage is designed as a learning tool for you to use when you reach your destiny.

Killing 101: What's the reward?

David's next step to his destiny involved him applying his experience as a killer and protector of sheep to the battle field. He had a habit of weighing his options to see if the risk was worth the reward.

The Israelite army was about to go to war with the army of the Philistines. There was a common practice in those days to have each army present their best warrior for a head to head fight; with the winner having his country declared the victor of the other country.

Goliath was the Philistine representative. He was a battle-hardened giant who had no fear. Whenever he would step forward and challenge the Israelites to give him someone to fight, the Israelites shrunk back in fear.

David sees what's going on and asks what the reward is for the person who kills Goliath. Even after one of his brother's gets mad at him for even thinking that he has a chance, David went and asked someone else what the reward was.

There are times in our lives where we know it's what we were called to do and the people who we think should support us don't. You have to be like David and continue to press on.

Having this giant make God's chosen people, David's fellow countrymen, look weak was intolerable to David and his heart was set on fixing the situation. Even though he was willing to get involved, he wanted to make sure he understood what the reward was.

This tactic is very useful in our everyday lives. We all have situations and argument that we want to be involved in because they aren't right; but you have to stop and see what the reward is.

Is it worth you arguing with someone if all you will accomplish is being able to say you won the argument? Is it worth spending hours on social media complaining about politics if you aren't able to actually have an effect on policy? Decide what you want to stand for and act on it in a productive way that makes a difference.

David didn't just jump into the fight. He knew that one reward was that he was fighting for God's good name. The other part of the reward was from the King himself: whoever killed Goliath would get riches from the King, marry the King's daughter and his family would be exempt from paying taxes.

Knowing exactly what you are fighting for will give you another advantage. If you are interested in fighting for God and things that are righteous in nature, your focus is good and you won't fail.

It's when you are more interested in fighting for a cultural group, corrupt legislation or greed is where your "risk vs. reward" factor is not in alignment with what God wants you to focus on and any victory in those contests will greatly alter your ability to be truly successful in life the way God intended.

Usually this means applying a particular set of skills, experience or resources that you have or are familiar with, to the cause. Sometimes you can learn as you go. That is where it's up to you to decide how committed you want to be. This leads us to David's next step towards his destiny:

Apply the strategy that fits you.

Once David decided the reward was worth the risk and he had confidence in his strategy, he didn't let anyone talk him out of it.

Have you ever decided that you felt led to do something a certain way, but when people tell you that you shouldn't do it that way, you change your plans? Your destiny is for you. Stand strong and know that even if it is good advice, it may not be the right advice for you. This is where your ability to hear from God and only God will keep you on your path to success.

David dealt with this same type of situation. Once the King heard David was going to battle, the King had David put on a bunch of heavy armor. This wasn't bad advice at all because whoever goes up against Goliath would need some protection; but David wasn't facing Goliath alone: from the beginning he felt that God was with him on this one.

A slingshot with some stones was David's weapon of choice. That's what he was familiar with and that's what he used to attack Goliath. David chose this weapon not only because of his familiarity with it, but also because using the slingshot was his best strategy.

Goliath was huge and had a heavy sword and was covered in metal body armor. Going toe-to-toe with someone like that is not as wise as being able to attack him at close range and still maintain your distance.

You know what your strategy is and why. It could be because you "just feel it", or because you have a love for it or because you believe the Holy Spirit led you to go a certain route. Whatever the reason is…stick with it. YOUR destiny is at stake…not anyone else's. Choose your weapons and strategy carefully and to increase your chances, learn to get advice on which strategy and weapons to employ from God.

David's strategy works and he kills Goliath.

Finish the Job

After Goliath falls to the ground, David approaches and then proceeded to cut off the dying man's head; keeping the head with him in a bag as a trophy.

David could have just stood over his fallen enemy and stabbed him in the heart or a number of other ways to make sure he was dead. Instead he chose to make a statement of finality.

When you face a problem, it feels good to follow it to completion. That's how you want to view each test in your life: don't just pass…get a straight "A".

If you are battling with any type of addiction, loneliness, rejection or depression you want to get to the point where there is absolutely no way an event or person can trigger you into a downward spiral.

Build your confidence up in God's promises to never leave you to the point where you know with an absolute surety that you are never alone and that as you follow God's laws He will never reject you. It's right there in the Bible:[11] "Be strong and courageous. Do not be afraid or terrified…for the LORD your God goes with you; He will never leave you nor forsake you."

Are you feeling like you're not able to live up to your natural feeling of destiny because of your present situations? Learn to study God's word to the point where you experience every experience of everyone in the Bible who clung to God's Word and rose above slavery, being tortured and anything else that was thrown in their way!!

God loves you the exact same way and the sooner you learn how He operates, the sooner you will understand that, like the scripture says[12] "For I am convinced that neither death nor life, neither angels nor demons, neither the present nor the future, nor any powers, neither height nor depth, nor anything else in all creation, will be able to separate us from the love of God that is in Christ Jesus our Lord."

First comes lust, then comes murder…

---

[11] Deuteronomy 31:6
[12] Romans 8:37-39

When you know what the rewards are, it is important to keep your concept of reward in line with what the Bible says. At any point and time, if you drop the ball, your life could be thrown off track. David was no exception.

He was on his rooftop and from where his viewpoint he was able to see a young lady taking a bath out on her rooftop. Curiosity got the best of him and he had one of his staffers find out who she was.

Upon learning that she was not only married, but she was married to one of his army officers, should have been enough reason to leave it alone. The risk-reward was not worth it. I have been in plenty of situations that any rational person would not get involved with. From the outside looking in it's always easy to say what you would or would not do. Who knows what was going on in David's head that day? Maybe he was lonely or just letting his brain relax.

Whatever the reason, he decided to pursue her and have sex with her. She got pregnant and now David had to begin the vicious cycle of covering up his sin.

He winds up having her husband, his faithful army officer, murdered. She now becomes his wife and they have a baby boy. It would appear as though he got away with 1st degree murder, but God sees everything. In this instance God decided to take the life of the child born from the lustful relationship.

There are times where we have done something stupid and did our best to cover it up. It may appear, like David had thought, that it's all good. The Bible shows us ALL aspects of God and one trait that is shown to us is that somehow God is able to see everything that everyone does.

With that in mind, we have to be ready for the consequences whether anyone knows or not. As you walk with God more and more, you will actually feel in your heart before you act, whether or not you should do something.

David was close with God and it is safe to assume that He knew what the right thing to do was, but he allowed lust to get him off track.

A commendable trait that David had was that when he did make a mistake he was more than willing to accept the punishment. When he heard that God was going to take the life of his son as punishment, David began to mourn and pray every day for his son's life. Once his son died, David got dressed, stopped mourning and it was business as usual again.

He understood there were consequences for his actions. That is where faith in God's judgment and being accountable to God is imperative. God will not always have death as a punishment, but we have to be prepared for, and accept, that[13] "…no discipline seems pleasant at the time, but painful. Later on, however, it produces a harvest

---

[13] Hebrews 12:11

of righteousness and peace for those who have been trained by it."

CHAPTER FOUR

King of Kings – Lessons from Jesus' life on Earth

Jesus life was designed to be the ultimate example of how we are supposed to live. He would talk to the people in a story-telling way that had lessons hidden in them. These stories are called parables. The other way He taught was by teaching them, and us, the importance and benefits of acting on what He says we should do. Here's what He told them, and us, to do and the benefits of doing it:

It's in the parable.

When Jesus taught lessons, he would speak in parables.[14] His rationale was that parables made it easier for people to understand and not just hear.

Let's look at the "gift horse" example. There is a saying that says "Never look a gift horse in the mouth". The meaning behind it is that when someone gives you a gift…just accept it. It's not polite to ask how much it cost.

This saying started during an era where horses were the main means of transportation and were one of the most valuable assets in society.

---

[14] Matthew 13:10 - 16

When you want to determine the value of a horse you look in its mouth. That is how you can see how healthy it is and how it's aging and then you can determine what a good price for it would be.

So if someone during that time period were to give you a horse as a gift, if you received it and began to look into its mouth you would in essence be trying to figure out how much it was worth and that would be rude; hence the saying "Never look a gift horse in the mouth."

That is how Jesus chose to operate. He talked to the people of that time period in ways they would understand. They primarily dealt with farming and livestock as the main forms of determining financial worth. Many of His lessons were along that line.

Here are some parables that dealt with issues that were common in the everyday lives of people back then; but still allow us today to see the lesson in it.[15]

Receiving God's Word:

The "Parable of the Sower" is a story about a farmer who planted some seeds. Some seeds landed on rocky ground, some on thorny ground and some on good soil.

Those farmers knew that seed on rocky ground would die because they wouldn't have stable ground for the roots to grow. This symbolized people who hear the Word

---

[15] All of the parables mentioned are found in the book of Matthews.

and are excited, but since they don't study the Word, when problems come, their faith soon dies off.

The seed on thorny ground that grew would eventually die from getting choked to death by the thorns. This symbolized people who hear the Word, but allow stress and life choke the life out of the power in the Word; killing their faith.

The seed that landed on the good soil grows and becomes a productive plant. This symbolized people who listen to the Word, study the Word and don't allow anything to stop or limit their productivity and enjoyment in life.

Applying Jesus' teachings to your everyday life:

The "Parable of the Wise and Foolish Builders" is a story about two men who each built a house.

The Wise Man built his house on a solid stone foundation. This symbolized how people are that listen to Jesus' teachings and apply them to their life. They aren't easily moved when life hits them. They have practiced the lessons from Jesus on how to handle stress and life and they continue to be productive and enjoy life.

The Foolish Man built his house on land that had sand in it. The natural weather and storms destroyed the house and it caved in. This symbolizes how people listen to the Word and build their life around it…but since they haven't actually applied the teachings to their lives they succumb to life's everyday struggles and don't get to experience true joy.

God the Father helping us when we get lost:

The "Parable of the Lost Sheep" tells about a shepherd who had 100 sheep. When he loses one, he will leave the 99 and go look for the missing one and when he finds it he is very happy.

This symbolizes how God the Father feels when one of us gets off track and He is able to guide us back on the path. He loves it! He created all of us and it's His desire to see that we all get to Heaven! He will come looking for you when you are lost.

This means that no matter how low you think you have sunken, He will go there in your darkest hour and do whatever it takes to help you get focused on your focus again.

That's why it's important to have people who study God's Word be in positions where they can be examples of Christianity and are trained in the ways of helping people who have gotten sidetracked. That is an important role in society.

Forgiving Others:

The "Parable of the Unmerciful Servant" is the story of a servant who owed a lot of money to his employer, the King. He asks for forgiveness and the King waives his entire debt.

The servant then turns around and presses one of his fellow servants for a small amount of money that was owed to him. The King finds out and gets mad. He tells the servant "I forgave you and you can't forgive the next man?" And then he issues a punishment, sending the man to the torture chambers until he finds a way to pay the King back the original debt that he owed.

This symbolizes how God the Father wants us to treat other people. He set a plan in motion to forgive us of ALL our sins that involved the killing of His only son; and in doing so, revealed to us the importance of forgiveness.

In return, he asks that we apply that same principle to people in our lives. He's not expecting us to forgive millions of people like He did…just the people we come across. If we are unwilling to do that, then we are showing ingratitude to Him and His teachings and He does not take that type of disrespect lightly.

Complaining Coworkers:

The "Parable of the Workers in the Vineyard" is a typical workplace story.

A man owned a vineyard and in the morning, he hired some guys to work that day. Everybody agreed to their day's wages and began to work.

Later on in the afternoon, the owner hired some more guys to work the last hour or so in the day. Everybody agreed to their day's wages and they too started to work.

When the day was over and it was time to get paid, the guys who worked the whole day just knew they would get paid more than the ones who only worked a couple of hours. But when they had seen that everybody got the same pay they began to complain.

So the owner asks the complaining workers "You agreed to a fair wage and so did they. Did I cheat you? Why are you worried about what I paid the other crew anyways?"

This story symbolized how we are supposed to be content with what we make. If we agree to an hourly wage or salary, then be happy with it. It's not your business to worry about what the next person gets or what the owner wants to do with his/her money.

Actions speaking louder than words:

The "Parable of the Two Sons" is a story about a dad who wanted his two sons to work the family business.

One son said "I don't want to" but later changed his mind and worked. The other son said "I will work for you" but didn't go.

Jesus said that the son who changed his mind and decided to work is the one who did what his dad asked and was productive. He related that to people who were caught in a life of sin and then heard the Word and decided to change their ways and do good. He said they will enter Heaven.

He told the religious leaders of the day that they were like the son who said he would work but didn't do anything. Jesus said this because the religious leaders knew what God required of them and they agreed to hold the positions…but they have acted as though they don't know the Word. They were unproductive because they didn't practice what they preached.

Being ready when the End of Times comes:

The story of "The Day and Hour Unknown" tells us about a servant who wasn't prepared for his master to come home.

Jesus gave the scenario of a man who left town, and while he was gone puts a servant in charge of the house. When the owner returns and the servant is still taking care of the owner's business matters he will be rewarded.

He then asked, "What if the servant who was left in charge decided to just drink and have a good time, and assumed that the owner would be gone for a while; and the owner comes home early?" Jesus then answered His own question by saying, "That servant will be severely punished and will lose all responsibilities he had."

This story was meant to symbolize the fact that we should always try and do the right thing. We don't know when Jesus will return or the world will end. We do know it will end. We do know Jesus will return. We don't know what day, so it would be to our benefit to live each day as though either Jesus will come or the world will end as we know it.

How to use what you have responsibly:

The "Parable of the Bags of Gold" is an example of two things. The first thing is how we will be rewarded based on our history of being productive; and the second thing how to use what we have productively

This story starts off with a man getting ready to go on a trip. He calls his servants in and proceeded to give one of them 5 bags of gold, another one got 2 bags of gold and the last one he gave 1 bag of gold. The gold was passed out based on their past responsibility records.

When he returns, he calls them in and asks how they did with the money he left them. The one who had 5 bags showed his boss that he now had 10 bags. The boss was happy. The second servant that had 2 bags showed his boss that he now had 4 bags. The boss was happy. The third servant explained that he didn't want to risk something happening with the 1 bag he was entrusted to, so he just dug a hole in the ground for safe keeping. The boss was not happy.

The boss tells the last servant "The least you could have done was to put the money in a bank so I could receive interest on it."

In disgust, the boss gives the bag the last servant had to the servant who started off with 5 bags. The servant who buried his bag gets kicked out of the house because, as the boss said, "He is worthless to me and lazy."

This symbolized that whoever has and is responsible will be given more. The person that doesn't have much will lose his little bit.

Some people say this parable is about money. That is partially true because it can be applied to someone with a lot of money: if you handle it rightly, you will be given more. On the flipside, if you are horrible with money, you will make poor financial decisions and eventually lose it all.

It doesn't end with just money though. When you have a lot of talent God expects you to use those skills for good. This story implies that you are given more (skills, talents, money, etc.) to use, the more you prove you are acting responsibly. This story also says, "Whoever has a lot will be given more and will always have an abundance to work with."

Parables Summary: These parables can have different meanings to different people. Some people view them literally; while other people focus on the principle behind the story. However you look at them, the main thing to remember is that these are Jesus' direct Words and that each one has at least one valuable lesson in it that makes it worthwhile to study.

Actions with Benefits

Jesus' life story is one big "how to". He tells us how to act in different scenarios and shows us the benefits of our actions.

There was a situation where Jesus had been talking to a crowd people and healing the ones who were sick. This went on all day. As it got late His disciples suggested that Jesus send everybody home so they could eat.

Benefit Story: Jesus told His disciples to give Him the food that the people there had on hand. It was five loaves of bread and two fish. He then gave thanks to His Heavenly Father and began to break the bread and fish up. In the end, all 5000 people were fed with 12 baskets of leftover food.

Benefit Lesson: Listen to what Jesus tells you and you will be able to be a blessing to people with what you have. You don't have to have a lot, as this example shows.

Benefit's Story[16]: Later on that night, Jesus told His disciples to get into the boat and He would meet them on

---

[16] The basic story about feeding the 5,000 remains the same in the books of Matthew, Mark and John regarding Jesus walking on the

the other side of the lake. They did what He said and when they were a ways out, they got caught in a horrible storm.

Jesus walked on the water out to the boat. At first they thought it was a ghost. Once Peter heard Jesus say "Relax, it's me", he said "If it's really you, then tell me to come to you on the water."

Jesus said "Come on." Peter stepped out of the boat and began to walk on the water; but as he looked around and saw the storm, he got scared and began to drown. Jesus reached out and saved him, asking him "Your lack of faith made you doubt what I said." They get into the boat and the storm died down and they continued to the other side as was the plan. Here are the benefit's lessons:

1. The first thing to look at is that Jesus told the disciples to start off across the lake towards the other side and that He would catch up with them later. A storm came up against them *but* they still made it to the other side. When Jesus tells you to do something and says He will always be with you…you will somehow *always* get where He needs and asks you to go on your path to your destiny.
2. The disciples set out across the lake at night time. The average person would be scared to death to cross a lake in the middle of the night. Jesus knew there were experienced fishermen in the boat. They

---

water. There are slight differences in the rest of the story but not enough to lose the accuracy in the Jesus part and that's why I included the story still.

weren't concerned with the story; in fact they had been battling it all night until Jesus came. When He sends you somewhere, He already knows your skills that you have and will need to use to get to where you need to be. That's why it's important to pay attention in life and learn from each experience and situation you come across. Build your expertise level up so God can use you for more and more things as you fulfill your destiny!

3. Their trek across the lake began at night time and even though they were getting tossed around in a storm, Jesus didn't head out to meet them until the early morning. We need to recognize the confidence level Jesus has in us to get to our destinations by continually following God's Word and experiencing God's goodness; building our confidence in what God says will happen! Jesus walked. He didn't rush out there and ask was everybody ok. He knew they would be ok.

4. Your works and actions will be directly related to the amount of faith you have as you step out towards your destiny. We often ask God to help us and then it is us who drops the ball. Peter asked Jesus to tell him to come out and walk on the water. Jesus gave him the green light and Peter actually walked on the water *until* he took his eyes off of Jesus and onto his situation. Even after Peter lost his focus, Jesus still saved him and got him back on track and we can expect Him to do the same for us.

Another scenario that may have different views on is the one with the fig tree. Jesus was with His disciples and was hungry so He walked over to a fig tree. When He discovered there were no figs on it, He cursed the tree and it died.

Benefit Story: Jesus used vines and trees a lot in His stories. He would say things like "I am the vine and you are the branches" or "judge a tree by its fruit." Keeping in line with that train of thought, I believe Jesus was mad at the tree for not producing what it was designed to produce.

He said "I am the vine and you are the branches and without me you can't survive." Another tree example was "I am the vine and my Father is the gardener. He prunes some branches but the ones that aren't producing He will cut off. The fig tree wasn't producing so it had no purpose."

Benefit Lesson: We are designed and created to love God. When we aren't being productive in the way He made us, I believe Jesus views us in the same way He viewed the fig tree with the only difference being we have salvation and that is our saving grace.

Benefit's Story: Jesus' act of dying on the cross gives us the ultimate "how to" as it relates to "talking the talk and walking the walk." He said the commandments can be summed up by: loving and respecting God and treating other people how you want to be treated. Respecting God means that we obey Him. Treating people how we want to be treated means that we forgiving others and we should be willing to lay down our life for them.

<u>Benefit's Summary</u>: He showed us how to obey God to the point where we are willing to do *whatever* God asks of us. He showed us how to forgive others by praying to His Heavenly Father to ask forgiveness for the people who had put Him on the cross. He showed us how to be willing to die for a righteous cause so that others may benefit.

He is truly deserving of the title King of Kings. He led by example. He acted in a dignified manner. He never compromised what He wanted for the sake of the people. He treated people fairly and the same regardless of their position in society. He carried out God's law in the land with blind justice. That is why ultimately all power and authority in Heaven and on Earth was put under His rule!

CHAPTER FIVE

Prince of Darkness - Lessons from observing Satan's tactics

Satan has been deceiving people for a long time. That's his work history. That's what he does.

Jesus said that Satan has no control over Him. We are brothers to Jesus and that means we also have this same ability. It's time to exercise our control. In order to effectively so battle with Satan, our common enemy, you have to know how he operates so that you can effectively maintain an offensive or defensive position against him. Satan's tactics exposed:

Thrust and Parry

"Thrust and parry" is a term that refers to the act of making an offensive move (thrusting a knife for instance) while avoiding offensive moves from the enemy (parrying). The Bible tells us over and over that we are in spiritual warfare with Satan and his followers.

His evil, deceptive and corrupt, but consistent, work history began in the Garden of Eden when he approached Eve to eat some fruit that God said her and Adam weren't supposed to.

Learning efficient counter-attacks and having strong defensive maneuvers are necessary when dealing with the enemy. We will begin our analysis of his work history beginning in the Garden of Eden to learn how to out-maneuver, attack and provide a strong defense when in combat with this enemy:

<u>Tactic 1</u>: When he has a choice of who to tempt, he will target the one who hasn't had the habitual daily walk history with God.

He knew Adam had been walking with God on a daily basis and hadn't eaten from the tree. Eve was newer on the scene and he approached her even though Adam was standing near her.

<u>Defensive Maneuver</u>: Get a strong work history of doing what God says and reaping the rewards. That way you will understand that when God tells you to do or not do something, you will get used to trusting Him and you will be less susceptible to temptation.

<u>Tactic 2</u>: He understands the power that "being like God" can have on a person. That wanting to "be like God" is what got him kicked out of Heaven.

<u>Defensive Maneuver</u>: Set your desire on wanting to God-like in your actions. The Bible repeatedly tells us not to be jealous of what someone else has or can do. Be content to submit to God's will. That is the *only* way we should want to be God-like.

Tactic 3: He understands the natural power of attraction and seduction that a woman has over a man and uses that to his advantage. The Bible tells us that a man will leave his parents for a female. There is a natural, built-in drive in a man to please and provide for a female.

In 1Corinthians 7, Paul recognizes this and says that it is a man's responsibility as a husband to sexually satisfy his wife when she wants. He then says sometimes it's best to stay single because a man will want to please his wife and that may get in the way of him pleasing God. Satan capitalizes on those natural urges and ways of a man.

Defensive Maneuver: A man has to be aware of the natural drive to please a female and make sure that drive doesn't override anything that would get in the way of him pleasing God.

A female has to be aware of the natural drive a man has to please her and she has to learn to channel that drive appropriately; with appropriately meaning: guide a man to please you as long as it doesn't interfere with his ability to please God.

That means men and women need to understand the Bible to the point where they know when their actions would cross the line and go against what God asks them to do.

Tactic 4: Satan hates us. He is willing to test our love for God to the extent that he will do whatever it takes…just to see how much we love God.

In the Book of Job, Satan had seen how faithful Job was to God and asked God to let him (Satan) do whatever he wanted to test Job's love for Him. He decided to take away Job's health, kill his family and take away all his wealth. All of that just to test someone's love for God.

<u>Defensive Maneuver:</u> The Bible teaches us that "God has plans for good for those who love Him." The deeper that concept is in your system, the more you will understand that life will have storms and ups and downs, but there will always be some sort of rhyme and reason for it.

You have to read stories in the Bible like Job or of King David and others who went through hard times. When you study their stories you will see how to get through the rough times and how God operated for their good.

The more instances where you see how God works, the more you will be able to relate your situation to someone else's who made it through. You will know that God operates and comes through for us in different ways and you will learn your part.

When God gave me business plans in my heart I was able to read the story of Joseph and keep my faith. In that story, Joseph was given a vision of greatness in a dream from God. He had a chance to tell some people to remember him when they spoke to the King.

When they got out of the jail they were all in, they forgot about him. Several years later, one of them had a situation that became an opportunity for him to mention Joseph. Joseph was then brought out of prison to council the King and the King loved his advice and instantly put him second in command of the country.

That story serves as a reminder for me. The main way is that when God gives you a dream, He will do it at just the right time. I had a tendency to want to share my vision with others so that I would get my chance to play it out.

Reflecting on Joseph's situation kept me focused and reminded me that all I had to do was wait for the opportunity to come my way. It gave me a confidence knowing how God had operated in a similar situation.

It gave me peace knowing that I didn't have to go out and "peddle" my ability and dreams. If any of you have dreams of greatness inside you, this story will help you understand your role. *THAT'S* the importance of reading and understanding these real life examples of people who loved God, understood how He works and were able to live out their dreams. It may take years, but if you know that it can take years to come into play, it will help you keep the faith.

Divide and Conquer

When you are in combat, one of the best ways to win is to scatter the enemy. Facing a united front is so much harder than facing an enemy whose frontline is scattered and broken.

Within the Christian religion there are dozens of different denominations. These are the results of some Christians interpreting a scripture differently than another group of Christians. Each "spin-off" creates a different denomination that has its own rules of conduct for its followers. It's gotten to the point where these "spin-offs" began to just say they are non-denominational.

How are Christians supposed to spread the Gospel when they find it hard to work together based on their view of how a Christian should live?

I honestly can't give Satan credit for this confusion. However, I do know from reading Bible stories that he has the ability to affect the way people think by baiting them. With that knowledge, I have seen how the allure of "pulpit power" can lead pastors away from their original intent or calling.

There is also evidence of this within the congregation itself. Pride is allowed to slip in and cause havoc. Certain members feel like they should have been promoted in the church above other members. This person doesn't feel like that person should be the new choir director so rumors begin to get spread.

Other times, as is the case in the United States of America, cultural groups have caused the great divide. The Bible was systematically used as a tool to support slavery by the majority white ruling class. As slavery was abolished, the minority black class began to adapt its own version of Christian practices in their worship services.

So now the Church as we know it today is divided based on culture and interpretation of scripture. I am inclined to say that this is due more to Christians not training and arming themselves properly with the knowledge in the Bible.

The Bible repeatedly tells us that we should learn patience. We should not be proud. We should practice humility. We should treat people how we want to be treated. We should come together as a Church and help other members.

If we began to actually live our lives the way we profess that we do (according to the Bible)…the Church would have a strong, united front and Satan would be facing an impenetrable wall instead of being able to maneuver freely through members within the Church body, weakening it at its core.

Control the Mountaintop

We have seen that Satan and his followers have the ability to influence people directly and indirectly. They know what our weaknesses are and can strategically place them in front of us. If we take the bait, it means our destruction, or at least it makes us ineffective at fighting them.

There is a common knowledge that in order to control any society, there are seven spheres of influence. These are: religion, family, education, government, media, arts & entertainment, and business. It's a safe bet assuming that Satan is aware of this.

Armed with this intelligence, you can see the need for people with experience in living right being in control of these areas. Let's take a look at each of these and see what condition the leaders have left them in:

Religion: The Church is so divided with infighting that a united front is more a dream than a reality.

Family: God intended the man to be the head of the family. Some men have allowed themselves to be taken out of the game; while outside forces have targeted other men to take them out of head-of-household status to disrupt the natural family structure.

Education: There is enough money for people to spend billions of dollars on business deals and porn-related activity…but no money to support quality education for anyone who wants and needs it. Lack of education will break down any society.

Government: The leaders in government are more interested in voting along party lines than voting for the best interest of the citizens. There is unjust legislation that targets the destruction breakdown of several, if not all, of the other mountaintops.

Media: Most major media companies spotlight every instance of injustice, death or destruction for news ratings to the point where most people believe the world is completely in disarray and the most horrible place in the Universe when in reality it's not.

Arts & Entertainment: People in these areas are often viewed as gods and as being above the law. When these people are able to be in the spotlight and make immorality look appealing…people are led away by all the glitz and glamour.

Business: Big business uses its wealth to corrupt politics on an everyday basis. The companies with the most wealth are more interested in controlling and hording the flow of money than they are in using it for the better of society.

I could go into a ton of detail, but I won't. You can clearly see how important it is that leaders in these seven areas are morally strong. You can clearly see where the lack of good values affects millions of people in the most negative ways.

These leaders have to understand the importance of money. These leaders have to understand the importance of the effect their image has on impressionable minds. These leaders have to apply, without prejudice, the "Golden Rule" concept which says "Treat people how you want to be treated." These leaders need to have proper training and instruction in how to behave properly before they leave Earth. These leaders need to understand how to battle Satan and his followers in these seven specific areas. These leaders need to be fully knowledgeable on true, loving behavior. These leaders need to receive the best warfare instructions as possible and from the best source available…the Bible: the "Basic Instructions Before Leaving Earth" manual!! Don't enter spiritual combat without it!!

CHAPTER SIX

Lessons Summary

I'm here. Now what?

Competitive events are like life with one major exception: you can choose to play a particular sport...you cannot choose to be born. You can gauge your skills and desire with the skills required to play a particular sport and then you get to decide whether or not you want to participate or not.

Your birth was decided by someone else. Now that you are here, how do you make the most out of this situation? Most of us seem to be preoccupied with freedom. The freedom to try new things. The freedom to enjoy this life. The freedom to understand our place in this universe. The freedom to discover our value and worth.

It is very important to understand your value. The source of this information will determine your quality of life and that is what we all want in the end: a good quality of life for us and the ones we love and we want to have our value recognized. That being said the best way on how to achieve *quality, value* and *love* needs to be determined.

If you allow your value to be based on things whose value can be manipulated, you will NEVER recognize your true value and purpose. These "things" can range from material possessions to the way that society defines success.

This view will keep you in a constant state of frustration because of the lack of consistency with the changing dollar values of your material things as well as the changing values and shifts in society. This frustration will block your focus and keep you from enjoying life.

Because of this, some people are lead to simply live by the code of: do what you have to in order to survive. This view is also the basis of a life of confusion and chaos.

This view is what allows the business owner to take his profits and hide them in tax shelters or spend money trying to buy favorable legislation.

This view is what allows a person to disrespect other people that don't go along with their way of living. Do you know how many people there are on this planet and how many different views there are?

In order to truly enjoy life and realize your potential and value, you have to follow a set of rules that don't change. A set of rules that apply equally to everyone regardless of their social, economic or cultural differences needs to be instilled. (And for the record, saying "I just love everyone and I let people do their thing and I do mine" is not a realistic way to live peacefully because of the aforementioned reason.)

Rules of Engagement

The best things in life have rules and the quality of those rules ultimately determines the value in life.

Imagine a basketball game where some players were able to disregard the shot-clock for one reason or another. Imagine a baseball game where some players were able to get 5 strikes instead of 3 for whatever reason. Sports and any competitive event as we know it would suck and cease to exist.

They say you don't appreciate hot unless you experience cold and that you can't appreciate love until you experience hate. In that same vein of thought, you often times don't appreciate life until you've experienced death on some level.

I said that last paragraph because your ability to enjoy life is determined on how well you understand the rules and how well you apply the rules. The rules are designed to help you find the beauty in life's ups and downs. The rules help you appreciate your value as it relates to people around you.

The next logical step would be to determine the quality of any particular set of rules. As you know, I am a Christian and I can only tell you about the set of rules that I have decided to follow that have given me the best results ever: the Bible.

The Bible's rules are designed to give you that freedom you desire. It gives you instructions on how to love yourself and people around you. It provides examples of everyday people who followed the rules and lived purpose-filled lives and those who rejected the instructions and succumbed to the pressures and temptations life can throw your way.

Who made these rules?

There is evidence everywhere you look that this world was not created by humans. That option is not even an option. Many theories have popped up only to be blown out of the water with basic fact-finding techniques and procedures.

The people in the Bible were no different than us in their belief that a higher being exists. It's the way that they chose to believe who this higher being is that made a difference in their lives.

It's natural for us to call on God. In moments of tragedy we ask God why did this happen. In times of great joy we thank God for blessing us.

I can only speak from my experience as to who I believe this God is and how this entity operates. It is my experience that the Bible provides the most logical, natural explanation of who God is.

The creation story makes absolute sense. It says we were made from dirt. When we die, our bodies decompose and basically become dirt.

The Bible teaches us that this entity called God is made up of three separate beings that all operate interchangeably under the name God. They are the Father, the Son and the Holy Spirit.

The Bible even takes the confusion out of who God is by explaining each entities role and function in our lives. When you dissect each of the player's roles it is evident that it makes perfect sense.

The Bible even provides examples of each of these beings existence in the everyday lives of humans. Even though these Bible characters lived thousands of years ago, there is historical and scientific evidence that validate the times, events and places mentioned in the Bible.

We all have what we call a "sixth sense" or that "inner voice" that we can't always explain; but we swear up and down exists. The Bible helps give a simple, clear logical explanation for that as well.

When we observe how the people in the Bible times acknowledged God, and how our great-great grandparents acknowledged this same God and how we now acknowledge this same God, the proof that this God exists the way that the Bible says is quite evident and undisputable.

The Bible also teaches us that this God has plans for our good. This is seen throughout the way the world was made. Every season, every plant, every animal, every natural element has a specific purpose in providing humans with life as we know it.

What now?

Now that you have hopefully seen real life examples of people who have followed the Bible and lived exciting lives, you will want to do the same.

It takes some people longer than others to get where they want to be in life and that's okay. I am literally just now getting to the point where I am creating new habits by following the rules in the Bible.

If you are looking to try something new, try and just follow one rule in the Bible. Try looking at one person's life and figure out how their belief in the God in the Bible changed their life for the better. Understand the principles behind time: things don't change in a day. Everything in life has planning and rules. Your life is no different.

These rules were made by the creator of this Earth. He would know best how to operate here. When the Earth was made, it wasn't made for any specific cultural group: it was simply made for humans.

Study the Bible and learn how to not let anything stand between you and your happiness. God has answers for your situations and these answers have passed the test of time and are found in the Bible.

God is consistent. God has always been consistent. God has been around forever. God explains who He is and how He operates the best He can with the Bible. You have read this book and seen how the Bible can help you.

The Bible eliminates any excuse you can come up with because it has the answers. It has the answer to being a former slave. It has the answer if you thing you are too young or too old. It has the answer for if you were born rich or poor. It has the answer whether you are a felon or not. THE BIBLE HAS THE ANSWERS.

What your view is on the Bible now will determine the quality of your life. You are in the position to be fully armed and ready to live life to the fullest. The only question that now needs to be answered is: How will your view affect your future? You have value and your view matters!

For those looking to learn more about the Bible, you need to look into the lost books of the Bible. The Bible is a summary of hundreds of scriptures. If all the scriptures were to be made into a book it would have to be about 15 inches thick. What happened is when publishing equipment came out, people wanted a book of scriptures. There were several meetings to determine which scriptural books should be included and which ones should be left out.

The scriptures that made the cut give us an excellent, historically-accurate version of creation, who God is, the life of Jesus and other moments in history. Basically it covers what the average person needs to know to get an average understanding of the information relayed in the Bible. BUT...

There is a book called the Book of Enoch which gives a lot more detail about the Nephilim. These were the giants mentioned in the Bible several times. Enoch is not some random person. There is historical proof of his existence and he is mentioned several times in the Bible as well.

In Genesis 6:4, there is mention of these giants as "being the giants who were on the Earth before and after the flood". In Numbers 13 where Moses sent some spies to go check out the Promised Land of Canaan, they came back and said "No can do! We strongly advise against trying to invade that land! There are giants there who probably look at us like we are small ants or grasshoppers…that's how big they are."

In our eyes it's easy for us to look at them and have sermons talking about how weak and scared the Israelites were once again BUT when you take a deeper look at the description of the giants from the Book of Enoch you will understand it better. These giants were man-eaters. They were part man and part fallen angel. They had supernatural strength and power. They were depicted as being over 30 feet tall! With that extra information let me ask you: how ready and willing would you be to fight them?

The Book of Enoch also sheds more detail on stories such as the David and Goliath fight. We are taught about David fighting a giant when he was only a teenager. The significance of that fight is magnified when you realize how big and powerful the giant actually was! If the giant were only about 10 or 12 feet tall, I can't imagine an entire army being scared to fight him and that's exactly what the

Bible said: the whole Israelite army was scared to go to war because the enemy had a giant on their squad.

With this extra information, once again, we can see how scared they would be if the giant was one like the Book of Enoch describes. Goliath was a man-eater! He was at least 30 feet tall! That's about the basic height of a person that would look at an average size man and view him as a grasshopper (a 12-foot man would not make me feel like I was small as an ant…would he make you feel that way?? How about somebody who is about 30 feet plus??)

Another interesting missing book is called the Book of Adam and Eve. This is actually a two-book series. This book helps tie in a ton of missing information that is helpful to better understanding creation, Adam and Eve and who Satan is.

This book helps us see how sad and lonely Adam and Eve were once they had to leave the Garden of Eden. Like I said before, if all of this information was in the Bible as we know it today, the size of the Bible would be completely impractical.

Reading that series answered a question I had about how did other people get on the Earth if Adam and Eve only had the set of twins we know as Cain and Abel. This book tells us that they had two sets of twins about two years apart. The first set of twins was a boy named Cain and his sister; while the younger set of twins was the boy named Abel and his sister.

To summarize this missing bit of the creation story: Cain was supposed to marry Abel's sister and Abel was supposed to get with Cain's twin sister. Once Cain killed Abel, he married his own sister and began to have kids with her and fill the area with humans. The Bible tells us in Genesis 4 that Adam and Eve had another son named Seth. When he got older he married Abel's twin sister and started to have a family and fill the area with humans. Doesn't that bit of information help you understand the Creation story a little more???

This book also chronicles many attempts and strategies of Satan in his attempt to kill humans. The hostility behind Satan's motivation is made clear in this book. This book also has examples of how the strategies Satan used (and uses) to lead people astray from God. It is INSANE the accounts of Satan's attempts to lead people astray!!! What's also crazy is how you can see a lot of these strategies in play in society today in business practices, music and especially areas dealing with sexuality.

The Bible tells us Satan was a great musician. This series takes it a little farther and shows how Satan used music to lead hundreds of people from worshipping God to worshipping him…even when they were directly warned that to do so would mean they would die.

When you listen to gospel/Christian music, you dance a certain way and your mood is energetic and loving and full of thoughts of God and his love. How do you dance to your favorite kind of music? Do you dance the same way to your music as you do in church? My mood and style of dancing is COMPLETELY differently when I hear some songs about straight up sex or bumpin' and grindin' as opposed to a song about how God's love will get me through hard times.

This book goes into details on how Satan instructed certain people to make a certain type of music that would "set the mood"...a mood of lust. Upon reading this information I instantly reflected on the effect music has on me. Back in the day when I would do my dirt, I would get amped up (and sometimes coked up) listening to Tupac or NWA. I also would go to parties and shoot dice and get into fights at clubs and get grind on females in the club when certain songs were played.

This book made it crystal clear how Satan loves to use music to influence our moods and get us to act in certain ways. Have you noticed how calm you are when you listen to piano music and how aggressive you get when you listen to certain rock and roll or rap songs? It all begins to make sense on being selective with the music you listen to.

The last book I will reference for you helped me see how Jesus was when He was younger is called Infancy of Jesus Christ. This book is historically accurate as well. It talks about the events and other miracles Jesus did as a young boy leading up to the miracle the Bible talks about where Jesus turned water into wine at the request of His mother Mary.

This book also helped me get a more personal understanding of the relationship Jesus had with His parents Joseph and Mary. For instance, when Mary asked Jesus to turn water to wine He got an attitude with her. This book goes into a lot more detail about how Mary would use Jesus' bathwater to heal people and how people would come to her because of how compassionate she was to help.

Seeing Mary in this light helped me understand why people would worship Mary today just like they did back in the days of Jesus. There are stories and accounts of people seeking out Mary so "she could heal them." In actuality, it was the power of her son Jesus doing all the healing. If only we would worship the creator over the creation as it relates to giving God glory…

I hope the additional reading of some of the lost books of the Bible will 1) help you get a better appreciation, love and respect for God the Father on a more personal and intimate level and 2) help you see clearer and understand deeper how relentlessly Satan wants you to not follow God's laws and what his motivation is. I also hope this book gives you the information you need to answer any additional questions you may have while studying and reading the Bible. Seeing through that fog is guaranteed to help you live a happier, fulfilling and successful life!

Take a look at the next section called "Private Matters" to see how your view matters regarding sex, relationships, the value of culture and other topics.

The Private Matters topics in this book are:

1. Cross-Culture Advantage - 95
2. Only God Can Judge Me - 100
3. Sperm: the Ultimate Seed - 105
4. A Woman's Worth - 109
5. Contribute with a Conscience - 113
6. Porn Industry 101 - 117
7. The Only Habit You Need to Succeed - 125

PRIVATE MATTERS

CROSS-CULTURE ADVANTAGE

Culture is a major part of being human. It is, at bare minimum, the common link between any two people. It gives a person pride in their country. It gives any given group in society a feeling of purpose and accomplishment. Culture is what gives you a basis for your existence. Cultural festivals are proud moments for anyone of the group being celebrated; especially when the celebration is world-wide.

For people without cultural identity, any cultural benefits are un-applicable to you. Characteristics of people in "culture-less" groups tend to be lack of motivation, anger, jealousy, stress, depression, isolation, self-hatred and their actions typically appear to have been programmed and controlled by negative outside forces.

The highest levels of joy and beauty in life can only be found in opposites. You appreciate summer's heat after experiencing winter's cool. You appreciate and strive for the feeling of being loved and acknowledged more so after being hated and ignored. Seeing the sun sets your mind on a different mentality after being able to shutdown and relax hours earlier under the cloak of darkness. Humanity began and exists because of opposites: the sexual actions and differences of a man and a woman. When you have no other connections to humans and feel isolated it's gratifying to be able to know and build on cultural connections to give you that feeling of being a part of something.

Culture is a major part of being human. It is, at bare minimum, the common link between any two people. When that bare minimum desire of humanity does not exist, purpose in life gets distorted.

The Bible introduces us to a new culture. A culture that is 100% positive. Something that is 100% means there is no room for anything else. It is full. It is complete; and in the case of the cross culture there is no room for negativity such as lack of motivation, anger, jealousy, stress, depression, isolation and self-hatred. This culture is symbolized by the cross. To be more specific: the act of Jesus dying on the cross. Welcome to Cross Culture.

Being a part of the Cross Culture has benefits with no liabilities. When you are a part of that culture, you interact with people differently. You don't judge someone based on their appearance, because you understand appearances don't determine achievable elevation in life. You understand that *everyone* has the same seed-potential as you. You are governed by laws that transcend every manmade law that is not based on or enforced with love.

The only outside influences in this culture is God. Your understanding of and getting into relationship with God is what gives members of this culture an advantage over any other cultural group. Every cultural group except for Cross Culture is limited by ethnicity or acceptance by a member of a certain ethnicity. Cross Culture is only limited by humanity without distinction. Meaning, each member is a distinct, valuable member of this culture with the only qualification being that you are a human.

Worldly kings and queens are crowned based on money and bloodlines. Cross Culture kings and queens are crowned at birth regardless of their economic status or bloodline at birth. Cross Culture members have the inalienable right by birth to be the first in a line of royalty in their bloodline at any point and time in their life.

Cross Culture kings and queens are proclaimed royalty by the creator of the universe…not by the amount of wealth his family has or by the inherited status of his or her parents. Money can be manipulated and so can royalty that is based on it; bloodlines have no bearing in determining admission to royalty of a Cross Culture member.

A Cross Culture member is only limited in life by his or her view on what Jesus did by dying on the cross: Your view matters.

BIBLE: Basic Instructions Before Leaving Earth

Personal Development Notes

ONLY GOD CAN JUDGE ME

It's a common tattoo and code of life: Only God Can Judge Me. Actually, that's the wrong way to live ***and*** that's not what God wants. If you live by that motto you are limiting your potential and that of your families and communities. Here are some views on judging that may help:

It's a natural reaction to judge:

We judge people's worth based on what they have or don't have

We judge people's mentality based on their cultural group

We judge people's skill/education level based on how they talk and dress

We judge an entire culture based on a couple of individuals of that cultural group

Just because it's a natural reaction doesn't mean it's the right reaction:

It's wrong to judge people's worth based on what they have or don't have

It's wrong to judge people's mentality based on their cultural group

It's wrong to judge people's skill/education level based on how they talk and dress

It's wrong to judge an entire culture based on a couple of individuals of that culture

God actually instructs us to judge each other; but to do it properly:

People love to quote how Jesus says "don't judge". What He *actually* does In Matthews 7:1 – 2 is gives us a warning about judging: if you judge someone you are opening yourself up to judgment; so if you judge someone harshly that's how they will judge you…if you judge with compassion they will judge you with compassion.

Jesus also said don't worry about a little problem your friend has while you got major problems. He says to take care of your house first and then you will be in the position to help other people.

In John 7:24 Jesus says "Stop judging by appearances".

In John 8:12 – 20, Jesus says "If I do judge, my judgment is valid because I stand with my Father so He is my witness and the law says you need the testimony of two people to be valid."

In John 5:30, Jesus says "My judgment is just because I'm not trying to judge you to please myself; instead I am judging based on what the Father says and to please Him."

Conclusion:

In some form or another we judge people. When done properly, judgment maintains integrity and order; when money and self-serving motives are behind the judgment the results are anger, chaos, hate and frustration.

Solutions:

Judging is a natural reaction and can be an excellent tool to grow ourselves and our communities if done properly. Start by taking a personal inventory of why you are where you are in life right now and judge yourself honestly. This will help you see your strengths and weaknesses.

What is your judging standard?

If you want to live by the laws of the world (laws that crush your spirit and are bad for your health),then you are free to get money however you can because you have to take care of yourself, your family and/or your business. The problem with that system is there is no order: sell drugs, rob, embezzle, kill, rape…whatever gets you money or makes you happy is okay. In that system you can't judge because there are no set rules.

If you want to live by the Bible laws (rules that help you physically and spiritually), then you have to think carefully before you make a move but the end rewards are higher. You can't rob/embezzle: zero chance of going to prison and being away from your family. You can't sell street drugs or pharmaceutical drugs: zero chance of going to prison and/or adding to the corruption in society.

You have the choice to make that decision on your own. This pastor in a Christian podcast said: when you do wrong you get your best results in the beginning; when you do right there is often a waiting period for your reward ***but*** that waiting period is always meant to make sure you will handle the rewards properly and at the same time, it fine tunes your physical and spiritual parts.

BIBLE: Basic Instructions Before Leaving Earth

Personal Development Notes

Sperm: The Ultimate Seed

Sperm is the ultimate seed simply because of its power and ability to create humans.

<u>Everything on this planet and in this universe was made for humans</u>:

The ground and water provide natural nutrition for plants.

Through the process of photosynthesis, plants make the air breathable for humans and through consumption provide the human body with every necessary nutrient it needs.

Every human cell in our body needs water and without it, a human would typically die within 3-4 days. The chemical make-up of water, H20, makes water the only natural liquid that the human body needs to replenish itself and survive.

If the Earth was closer or farther away from the Sun…we would all die and if the Earth was to move faster or slower…we would all die.

<u>Humans are the most powerful life force on this planet</u>:

No other life form can control its environment like humans.

Nothing that is unnatural would have existed without humans: cars, boats, bridges, computers, etc.

No other life form has the ability to manipulate every element on this planet to its will.

On the spiritual side of things:

No other life form has a spiritual level comparable to humans.

No other life form has the ability to control its spiritual destiny.

Humans are the image of God.

A man's body is the only life-form that produces semen, the seed of humanity. The following are some of the activities that are designed to weaken a man or woman, stripping the ultimate power-couple of the proper use and function of this valuable seed:

Lust: Masturbating/jacking is a waste of seed/power

Contraceptives/"Safe" sex practices: They are counterproductive to married couples because responsible, natural fatherhood truest form of natural power for a man. They kill the potential of the seed/life

Abortion: Destroys the females body and kills the most powerful life form that exists

Homosexual relationships: These relationships disregard the natural function and wiring of a man and a woman;

causing confusion in the natural roles and functions of a man and a woman in the family.

Seeds are important. Jesus said "If you have faith the size of a mustard seed you can move mountains." When God created the Earth, He told man "I give you every seed-bearing fruit for you and the animals to eat." Every natural, living thing comes from a seed.

<u>For men</u>: You have power. Learn the correct way to utilize your seed's power and potential.

<u>For women</u>: You have power. Learn the correct process to select and utilize the power of a man and his seed.

<u>For parents</u>: You have power. Learn the correct way to nourish your seed to maximize its hidden potential.

BIBLE: Basic Instructions Before Leaving Earth

Personal Development Notes

A WOMAN'S WORTH

The Bible has several examples of how a woman can use her natural power and the results she can command:

Intentional use of Power: Jacob's mother used her female power of persuasion to help him deceive his father; Esther used her beauty and charm to become a queen and save her Jewish culture from genocide; the daughter of Herodias used her feminine sexual power of persuasion to have a man murdered; King David was about to kill a man and all the man's sons for disrespecting him but the man's wife stepped in and appeased David and saved her husband's life; God was going to kill Moses until his wife stepped in and did what God had wanted and that act saved Moses' life; and then there was King Solomon who asked God for wisdom over everything and in the end he allowed his wives to lead him astray to the point where he built temples for them to worship foreign gods and idols.

Unintentional use of Power: King David *looked* at a woman and wanted her so bad that he had her husband murdered; Jacob saw a beautiful female and told her dad that he would work for him for free for 7 years if he could marry her…he was tricked and forced to marry her older sister, but he went and told the dad he would *still* work for 7 more years if he could marry the younger sister who he wanted in the beginning; in Genesis it was told that the angels in Heaven *looked* down at the women on Earth and wanted them so badly that they would rather live on Earth and have them than live in Heaven; and finally, David had a son who lusted after his own step-sister so badly that he became physically sick and eventually raped her.

Understanding the worth of a woman and her role in a man's life is crucial, both from the man's point of view and the woman's. On several occasions God warned different men about their selection of a wife because if a wife doesn't love God, she has the power to lead her husband away from God. The first example of this was in the Garden of Eden.

The apostle Paul says that sometimes it's best if a man stays single because a married man has a hard time pleasing God because of his strong, natural desire to please his wife.

At the same time, the Bible mentions how a man should find a good wife because she will complement him and they will both be happy and powerful. In the Garden of Eden, Eve was created because God determined that Adam needed a female companion to complete him.

Here are some Bible verses that talk some more about a woman's worth:

1. Proverbs 11:16 – a kindhearted woman gains honor
2. Genesis 2:24 – a man will leave his parents to be with a woman
3. Proverbs 31:10-31 – a wife of noble character is: worth more than rubies, she has strength and dignity, gives good advice, helps the poor and deserves honor for everything that she does…

4. Proverbs 18:22 - Whoever finds a wife finds something that is good and receives favor from God.
5. Psalm 68:5 – God is a protector of widows
6. Exodus 22:22 – God says He will kill anyone who takes advantage of widows
7. Proverbs 12:24 – a disgraceful wife is like decay in her husband's bones
8. Proverbs 19:13 – a quarrelsome wife is like a constant drip from a leaky roof
9. Proverbs 29:3 – whoever messes with prostitutes will be poor
10. Proverbs 6:26 – an adulterous wife will cost you your life
11. Ecclesiastes 7:26 – thoughts of getting trapped by a woman are worse than contemplating death

In the end, a woman has the ability to support life or death. She needs no weapons of war. Her mind, beauty and natural feminine qualities are her weapons of choice. How a woman follows instructions and where she gets her instructions from determines her worth and value.

BIBLE: Basic Instructions Before Leaving Earth

Personal Development Notes

CONTRIBUTE WITH A CONSCIENCE

Some roadblocks to learning are unavoidable and to be expected; as is the case with "Generational Wisdom":

- People born during the beginning of the Automobile Era of the 1920's can't fully relate with people who lived during the Horse and Buggy Era; but both eras existed. The new Automobile Era people couldn't relate to the wild tales of the Pony Express.
- People born during the Advanced Automobile Era of the 1960's cannot fully relate to the previous Automobile Era people; but both eras existed. The earlier generations didn't even have speed limit signs; while later generations had to install computer chips in the engines so certain cars couldn't reach their max speeds of over 150mph during typical city/highway driving in certain countries.
- During the various eras of the Roman Caesar's, George Washington Carver and Thomas Edison, their world-changing inventions and political styles were absolutely remarkable…during those eras. Nowadays we flip on light switches, regularly purchase peanut-made products and navigate through our Roman-ideology based political system without a second thought.
- Each generation takes the collaborated technologies and life lessons from the previous generations to

determine the quality of life for their current generation to live in.

Conclusion: Typically, generational wisdom is at its zenith during that particular generation only. The morality of each generation's "Rule Setter's", major contributor's and their contributions determines not only that generation's quality of life, but it will also be the main ingredient for the next generation to build off of. Since history has shown us that the *morality* factor is the predominant and most necessary force in determining quality of life, I think that each generation owes it to themselves and future generations to make the creation of an unwavering, unapologetic and unprejudiced morally correct code of conduct be top priority for EVERY individual in EVERY aspect of our social, religious, political, corporate and personal lives be made a requirement…not a request!!

Debate/Discussion Questions:

- Do you disagree or agree with the premise that the moral code has more impact on society than the various contributions themselves?
- How well does the moral code "Just Love Everybody" work regarding personal choices with sex, occupation, guns and drug/alcohol use?
- Defend a religion's moral code by citing examples of societal problems that could have been either eliminated or minimized had the rules of that religion been adhered to. You must defend your

examples based solely on references from that religion's "hand book"...not current laws or emotions.
- Knowing that roadblocks to transferring generational wisdom exists, find ways to make the moral codes of "Bible Time" days relevant to our modern day culture.

BIBLE: Basic Instructions Before Leaving Earth

Personal Development Notes

PORN INDUSTRY 101

The porn industry is a home wrecker and a relationship killer. The porn industry is a career-killer. The porn industry is manhood-killer. How do I know? Because I used to love porn industry activity and it took the life out of my dreams, health and any thoughts of me being purposeful to anyone in life.

From reading the different stories in the Bible you can see how sex and lust affected many people's lives negatively…just like it does today. It made King David, a great Man of God, commit 1st degree murder. A King was willing to give up half of his kingdom for a lap dance. These may be situations that occurred a long time ago, but I am sure we all know, or are that person, who has made some dumb decisions because we allowed sex and lust to be the deciding factors.

The porn industry is an industry that faithfully reaps in several billion dollars a year with no signs of slowing down. IF YOU DO NOT GET A HANDLE ON YOUR SEXUAL DESIRES AND EXPECTATIONS, THIS INDUSTRY WILL CONTINUE TO TEAR UP HOME LIVES AND KILL DREAMS.

Sex sells. I have seen commercials for cookies that show a sexxxy female dancing around with some tight, fitting jeans on and some cleavage showing talking about how much she loves milk and cookies. I am lactose intolerant and I almost went out to buy some milk and cookies because they made it seem like if I presented a snack of milk and cookies to a female that she would somehow, in anticipation of me bringing her this snack, be waiting around in some sexxxy jeans or a nice short skirt knowing that I was on the way with her favorite: milk and cookies.

I believe that females that willingly participate in this industry are co-conspirators in aiding the sins of lust and misplaced sexual tendencies and desires.

Some females rationalize their actions by saying they are making money to raise their child. So are you saying that the immorality of the industry that you are supporting and the negative impact on society doesn't matter as long as you are taking care of your child?

Another common view is that they feel like they might as well get that money because the guy caught in that sad lifestyle is going to spend his money regardless with someone…so why not me?

How a female views the porn industry is not my expertise. In this Town Hall Topic I have to stick with what I know and that is strictly from the side of a paying customer. As a man, I can only give it to you from a man's point of view; and to be more specific I can only share my point of view. And to keep things simple, I will use the term "porn-activity" to refer to watching pornos, strippers and dabbling with escorts/prostitutes interchangeably.

Lucky for you, we are about to pull back the curtain and see how this industry can, and needs to be, brought to its knees. Here's how it got me:

Home Wrecker/Relationship Killer – Porn activity females are not portraying their nurturing, wifely, motherly sides. They show every side *except* those sides. This all appears harmless enough, but the more you watch and get involved, the more you begin to view women as simply sex objects. And why not??? They appear to be so happy and willing and as a man, you naturally want to keep a female happy.

1. The more accustomed I was to fantasy women, the less I was able to deal with a real woman. I was able to have all my basic female needs taken care of without all the talking and commitment.
2. Women I talked to said they would never consider marriage to a man who was involved in porn-activity because they know they can't compete with a female in that industry.
3. I got addicted to cocaine. Drugs and alcohol put you in a state of temporary "happiness". Cocaine kept my fantasy sex life alive; while killing any hopes of having a real relationship with a normal sex life.
4. The more my failures at having a real relationship grew because of my drug addiction and shame, the more my attempts to get in relationships did long-lasting damage to my girlfriends and the children that were the result of these relationships.

Career Killer – Having a career for me was out of the question. For each person this may be different. I allowed porn-activity to kill my career dreams and goals because of my inability to deal with real life.

1. I longed to be in a relationship so bad that I got high to enjoy my fantasy relationship any chance I could. Having a career and a drug addiction don't mix.
2. It became harder and harder for me to see myself in a real career achieving real results when I had no confidence in my dealings with reality.
3. It's hard to realize your dreams of being a big-time business owner and investor when you spend your savings on porn-related activities.

Manhood Killer – Becoming a man, like anything else in life, is the results of your habits. My habits were stripping me of my confidence and manhood with each bad decision. Having a man as the head of the house is the way God designed it. When you have a man who doesn't understand the job requirements of that position…the whole house is negatively affected and out of natural order; forcing the woman to be the mommy and the daddy.

1. A man respects a woman. The porn industry teaches men to treat women with disrespect, wanting them only as sex objects.
2. A man knows, understands and strives to live out the God-given guidelines for how a man is to conduct himself at all times. A man who is involved with porn-activity acts contrary to these rules. He becomes selfish and puts his needs and desires over those of his family, rendering him

useless as the proper head of a strong family unit. He allows substitutes to step in and fulfill his duties.
3. A man knows how to handle reality. The porn industry teaches men to sacrifice reality for fantasy. Reality can be tough. A real man has the confidence to accept the consequences of his actions. He does not have time to deal with fantasies because life if a blessing and is a reality. Operating in fantasy-land is counterproductive to being a good father or any other naturally ordained male role in both society and the home.
4. A man knows how to budget his finances. Budgeting money for sexual fantasies is not practical or wise. A man accustomed to getting his way sexually by using his money if a fool. In the end he is the one who is getting used. Even if he has enough money to take care of his home and his fantasy life, he is learning to use money to be selfish, immoral, undisciplined…all negative traits that rollover into other areas of his life.
5. A man loves commitment. The porn industry wants men to constantly be on the lookout for new and exciting sexual experiences. The porn industry allows a man to "live out" any sexual fantasy he wants. With so many porn websites and strip-clubs around, that type of guy has access to sexual fantasies 24/7 at the touch of a button or a quick trip to the local strip club.

There is a point in your life where it becomes harder to go back to the way it was. Kind of like a cucumber: once it becomes a pickle…it can't be a cucumber anymore. Your life is the sum results of habits. Bad sexual habits are hard to break. Somebody acted towards you based on the habits they were taught or you acted the way you did based on your habits.

The Bible teaches us and shows us and warns us about sex. It shows us how to create good habits that positively affect our sex lives and put us in good relationships. It also provides us with plenty of examples that show the good and the bad sides of our sex habits.

Sex was designed to be a beautiful act that compliments the natural attraction between a man and a woman to create children. We wouldn't be here without it. Our ability to enjoy life depends on our ability to enjoy sex the way it was meant to be. That's my new view and I'm stickin' to it.

BIBLE: Basic Instructions Before Leaving Earth

Personal Development Notes

THE ONLY HABIT YOU NEED TO SUCCEED

In order for any formula to be successful it must be able to be applied and used to anyone and any situation it was designed for. The formula for success is no different.

Nature provides us with many examples of true, unbiased formulas. Look at the properties of water: if you take a glass of water and turn it sideways…water will run out. It doesn't matter if you are black, white, short, or tall, fat or skinny…it will always run out. I think you get my point without me having to go into examples of gravity, rain and evaporation.

Rules are essential for life. Everything about life is built around rules. Successful people know the rules and live by them…that is what makes them successful. Here's the problem: people try to change the rules for their benefit. Once that is done, that rule is no longer a valid rule. It's as useful as a pocket with holes in it.

Sporting activities have rules that seem to be the fairest. The process to get on a team or into an event may be manipulated, but once on the court or the field the rules apply to each player equally.

There was a time in America when the entry process and the actual playing process was tainted and sports suffered as a result of it. Once the officials and prejudicial people hiding behind the scenes were able to see the benefit and rightfulness of applying the rules equally is when sports became the billion dollar entertainment industries they are today.

Businesses that want to influence politics for their benefit use money to corrupt the rules. They pay politicians and legislators to create and pass legislation that favors their industry; often times regardless of the health hazards or resulting financial injustices that come from said legislation. We see this horrible, common practice applied in industries such as banking and sugar just to name a couple of guilty parties.

Rules are so essential that people will risk their good name, their spiritual happiness, their career and spend millions of dollars *just* to be able to bend the rules in their favor. That's because they understand that rules are what makes the world go round, and if they can manipulate the rules in their areas of interest, they will be "successful".

Here's the thing about rules: the best rules favor any and everyone equally! The best rules are highly profitable and beneficial to all members in any given society! ANY type of manipulation in the process of creating or enforcing the rules will always have a negative effect and will be absolutely unproductive in the end.

Now we get to the part where you find out about this "one rule you need to succeed" thing. Well, drum roll please.......: **FOLLOW GOD'S LAWS IN THE BIBLE!**

That's it and that's all. Following the rules in the Bible is your advantage in life. If there is a law that applies to one culture or economic class but not another…following God's laws will help you get through the corruption to get to your destiny. If there is a law that is designed to keep certain people out of an industry or acts as a glass ceiling…following God's laws will help you get through the corruption to get to your destiny.

The instructions in the Bible are extremely simple to follow and everyone has access to them 24/7…even without advanced education or training, WIFI or internet access. Here's how it works:

Easy access: God said "I will write these laws in their hearts and minds". Once you understand that all law and order that comes naturally to you has a purpose and was placed inside you by the Creator of the universe…you can begin to understand that nobody is superior to you value wise. Someone may be a better athlete in a certain sport or better at accounting than you; but that only makes them more valuable than you in that particular arena…NOT IN LIFE.

Every one of us knows when we are doing something wrong. We somehow feel it inside that we are breaking some type of rule. The evidence is usually that the other person is sad or at a perceived disadvantage because of our actions.

We can either change our actions or change the rules. The easy, corrupt way is to manipulate the rules so that we can continue to have a perceived advantage over someone else for our benefit. By making certain activities or actions "legal", people learn to justify the deception in their character by saying "well, it's legal." If ANY manmade law goes against God's Law it is NEVER going to be legal. I say "perceived" because any "advantage" that is forged out of trickery or deception isn't an advantage at all. In fact, it puts the deceptive ones at a disadvantage because they are living a life based on intentional lies and deception.

The rules defined: Jesus said the rules of life can be summed up by simply loving and respecting God and treating people how you want to be treated. How do you show that you love someone? You find out what makes them happy and you perform that act as much as possible.

God made this Earth specifically for humans so it doesn't make sense to think He doesn't love us! If He didn't love us, He would've made gravity 10x stronger than it is and we would all be dragging our feet on the ground, unable to walk or move. Plants that have stronger and healthier healing power than any medicine made or sold in the pharmaceutical markets would not exist if God didn't love us.

The other half of the "rule's equation" is treating people how you want to be treated. Would you want someone to tell you or your child that you can't go to a certain college because of your cultural group? Most likely not…so don't make those types of rules. The whole Civil Rights Era could have been avoided by following that one, simple Bible principle.

The guaranteed path to success: In the book of Genesis, God told Abraham "Because you obeyed me, I will make you great…your descendants will take possessions of the cities of their enemies…" God said He would help Abraham's descendants take over enemy territories and would make his name great. All Abraham did was obey what God told him to do. He did one major act to obey God and God made that huge promise to him.

When the Israelites were going to be led by God to their Promised Land, God said "In order to get there and enjoy everything life has to offer…all you have to do is obey my commands." He never said that you have to all get college degrees or come from certain backgrounds…simply follow His commands.

In the book of Joshua we learn how Joshua's success in life was locked in. God told him "Obey my laws and you will have success wherever you go…no enemy will be able to stand against you…constantly think about these laws so that you can make good decisions…"

The word "enemy" is defined as: someone or something that tries to harm you or go against you. In the Bible, God was quick to let someone know that He would help them defeat their enemies. The enemies in these times were typically other countries that were at war with the Israelites or against any person that God supported.

I believe that same principle can be applied today to mean: anything or anyone who is against you or tries to harm you. That means if you obey God's laws that no type of legislation or rules that are deceptive in nature and meant to harm or be a stumbling block in your life will be successful.

<u>Summary of the only habit you need to succeed:</u> OBEY GOD'S RULES. Get into the Bible and apply any of the rules God gave. You can see the importance of rules and law and order in society, so follow the rules that give you the most freedom to enjoy life without encroaching on someone else's freedom to do the same. In your industry, treat people how you want to be treated. Don't be a part of anything or anyone who supports laws that are contrary to the Bible. Focus on these laws habitually. These laws need to be studied in some shape or form *every day*.

Continue to understand and value your success and the proper way to get it. Understand that your personal value is not at stake but your personal level of success is. And as your success level in life rises, so does the success level of people around you. **EVERY SINGLE RULE IN THE BIBLE IS DESIGNED FOR YOUR HAPPINESS AND SUCCESS AND AS A WIN-WIN FOR EVERYONE AFFECTED BY ITS APPLICATION AND ENFORCEMENT!!**

BIBLE: Basic Instructions Before Leaving Earth

Personal Development Notes

Made in the USA
Columbia, SC
18 July 2021